My Life as it Stands

Sharol Kelly

Contents

Dedication

This book is dedicated to my children and my family. They didn't always agree with me, but they stood by me and supported my decisions.

This book is also written for people who have addictions and for women who have been exploited by men. Hopefully, this book will protect women so they don't go down the same path that I did.

(Exploiter: a user of people for their own gain; they are selfish and take advantage of the vulnerable; they always use their opponent's weaknesses.)

I couldn't have written this book without the help of my sister Suzi, who loves to type. Thank you

Some names have been changed.

Preface

This is the story of my life and the mistakes I made and how I overcame them, which will include more specific parts of my life, including my oldest son Bobby Temple who was addicted to heroin. It also includes the marriage to my first husband, Jace, who I found out later was a pedophile.

I'll also be going into my life-changing experiences more in-depth with my third husband, Alva, who I thought was my dream husband. He turned out to be a con man and a murderer.

A big part of my story tells about felons behind bars who take advantage of vulnerable women. They mesmerize and hypnotize you and shower you with "love." They give you a feeling of confidence and self-worth. In reality, they are robbing and killing your soul.

Chapter 1: My Beginnings

I was born a Hoosier in Marion, Indiana, on June 22, 1946. When I was four years old, my dad was a truck driver who got transferred to Columbus, Ohio, as the manager. We moved one block away from The Ohio State Fairgrounds. The neighbors told us about parking cars for the fairgoers. We all charged fifty cents a car.

I had three older sisters: Arline, Suzi, and Kay. When I was four, they were fifteen, twelve, and seven. I was the baby and I got coddled by my two oldest sisters. They played with me, rocked me, sang to me, and took me outside and pulled me in our little red wagon. Maybe they were playing house with me. They did all this because they wanted to, not because they had to. They included Kay when she would let them. She was shy and a lot of times liked to play by herself.

Growing up, Kay and I were very close, but I'm sure I got on her nerves sometimes. When I started my menstrual periods, she told me why and what they meant. She also told me that when a woman fell in love, she would get married and then have babies. I always wondered how teenage girls had such cute boyfriends. I finally thought I figured it out, and it was because of sex without worrying about having children since none of them were married.

My parents were good to all of us, even though they didn't give us hugs or kisses or verbal expressions of love. When I was quite older, I realized how much they truly loved us. Even though they never talked about relationships with boys, sex, periods, or any "girl talk," I think it was due to the era in which they were born, in 1912 and 1914.

When I was around eight years old, I asked my mother if I could get a baby duck for Easter. She finally gave in, and I got what I wanted. It was a pretty yellow color and was so cute. We called my new pet "Gluck the City Duck."

When my mother was in the backyard hanging up her laundry on the clothesline, Gluck followed her around; she thought this was cute, and she really liked him. My mother wanted me to write a children's book about Gluck the City Duck, but I never got around to it. Now I wish I had written it.

Around the age of twelve, I told my mother I didn't feel loved. She took me to a psychiatrist. He asked me what was going on, and when I told him he had very little to say. My mother said that I knew that she and my dad loved me. I felt so hurt and guilty to see my mother upset. I never mentioned it again and wouldn't go back for any future visits to the psychiatrist. That's when I started to block my feelings. I didn't want to upset anyone with what I then perceived as my useless thoughts. I wanted love, not alienation.

Chapter 2:
Tragedies in My Young Life

When I was eleven years old, I went to a teenage dance at a local church with my sister Kay, who was fourteen years old at the time. I had to beg my mother to let me go, and she finally said I could go, but Kay would have to watch me. Kay said she would take care of me because she really wanted me to go so she wouldn't have to go alone. At the time, I wanted to be older so I could have more fun. There were a lot of couples slow dancing, and I was so envious. Seeing Kay dancing surprised me because she was really shy.

A few boys looked around fourteen years old, but some of them looked to be a couple years older. I had on a dress since, as girls, we could only wear dresses to school and church. I was sitting by the dance floor watching the dancers and listening to the music when an older boy asked me if I wanted to take a walk with him. I was so happy because I thought this was the first step in getting a boyfriend. He didn't say much when we were walking, and he didn't say much when he took my panties off and raped me. I didn't know this was wrong until two other boys came along and also raped me. Then I started thinking that this whole scenario was planned. Later on in the week, there was another dance. As I was walking into the dance, the second boy of the three boys asked me to go to his car to talk. I went because I thought he wanted to apologize for raping me a few days earlier. I suddenly realized it was for more than a conversation. He raped me again. I felt so ugly and dirty. And guilty. I even thought it was my fault.

I heard some yelling and clapping. I looked up through the windshield and saw around six fraternity guys sitting on a little deck watching. They were clapping and laughing at us (me) having sex. I was only eleven and I was so humiliated and sad. The guy with me in the car started laughing with them. I was so embarrassed, I felt so ugly, and I was confused. I never went back to the church dance again. My sister had no idea what had happened to me, and I didn't tell her until a week or so later. She wondered why I didn't tell her what happened to me before. She seemed very upset. We never mentioned it again. I felt so ashamed and depressed. Kay told me as my educator that I should never let any guy tell me any crap, that I didn't owe anybody anything. It seemed like she knew what had happened to me, so I questioned her, but she said she didn't.

After I had been taken advantage of, I met my first boyfriend, Wally, at the local skating rink. My friend Patty introduced us. Wally and I started Junior High School the same year and at the same school. I was very shy and didn't know who I could trust. It was 1959, and I was in homeroom. I felt incredibly uncomfortable that the black kids were on one side of the room and the white kids were on the other side. I knew nothing about racism and prejudice. Growing up, my parents didn't talk much about race. I'm not sure if that was just the times we lived in or if they didn't care much about racism.

When I was in the ninth grade, Wally and I had broken up (like on and off.) One time when I was in homeroom, I was struggling with a math problem. An African American boy named Leo came over to the white side of the room and asked if he could help me, and I said yes. That was the first time I met Leo, and I had feelings for him instantly. After I got to know him, my feelings grew stronger. I can only say good things about him. He was tall, dark, and handsome. He was kind, smart, and honest. Leo and I were talking one time about how some people thought blacks and whites shouldn't mix. I saw no difference between the races. We remained friends all three years of junior high school. He would walk two or three miles to meet me in my backyard at night. I would always make sure my parents were in bed, asleep. I remember one time he wanted to kiss me goodbye, and I had to stand on a crate to be tall enough to kiss him. We started our relationship as friends, and that's important. We also ended our relationship as friends.

Another incident happened to me in the summer of that year. I was babysitting for five children while the parents went to church. I was sitting in the kitchen listening to the radio when the father of the children came home from church early because he had to go to work, and he forgot his lunch. He said his wife would be home in an hour and I could leave then. He asked me if I liked to dance, and I said no, hoping he would leave soon. I had a bad feeling while he was there. He pulled me out of the chair and tried to get me to dance. I tried to get away and he got very rough. We were scuffling around, and I got very worn out. He laid me on the floor and raped me. I was too tired and scared to fight him anymore. He was saying weird things, such as "You're enjoying this. I'll get you to babysit all the time and we can do this again." I thought: *he's crazy*, and while he was talking, I was crying and begging him to let me get up. My dress was torn, and I was bleeding. He left, and I felt like leaving too. I was so upset but I knew there were five children asleep upstairs, so I couldn't leave. I talked to several friends, but the only one who offered to walk me home was my friend Leo. He had to walk two or three miles in alleyways to walk me home a few miles away, as he had walked that way before when we met in my backyard. Leo made me feel secure and safe, and even if we were just friends, I felt that I was loved. I was scared and I needed all those things to calm me down.

I was so scared of telling my parents because I was afraid my dad would go to that house and get hurt. Two months later, my period was late, so I knew I needed to tell my mother. She told my father, and he cried. Nothing else was ever done. I did have my period a few days later. Even though the guy involved told me he had surgery and couldn't get anyone pregnant, I was still afraid. Having my period start was lucky for me and convenient for him. I never went back there to babysit.

Another incident happened to me at that age. My friend Beth and I decided to go to a party at a friend's house. We both had to sneak out of our houses and ride the city bus to get there. We were going to take the bus to get home, too, but we didn't know the busses stopped running at 8 p.m. We didn't have a way home, and we couldn't call our parents, as they would be furious if they found out where we were, though Beth's mother didn't have any strict rules for her. I called Leo and asked him if he knew anyone that had a car who could pick us up. He found two older guys in his neighborhood who said they would do it. Leo came with them, so I sat in the back seat with him. Beth sat in the front seat in between the two guys. One of the guys pulled out some beer from under the front seat, and they passed it back and forth between the two of them. Leo refused to drink, as he was only fifteen, and looked so surprised that they were drinking.

Leo was also surprised when the driver went to a secluded area. Then the driver and the other guy raped Beth. She told them No, but they didn't care. Leo whispered to me to keep quiet because they knew I was his girlfriend, so he thought they wouldn't bother me. I was so scared that I was shaking. I was more afraid of being caught than being raped. It was around 1960, and black and white people together was not accepted back then.

Leo was really upset about what happened and kept apologizing. He had no idea something like this would happen. There was nothing he could have done to stop them. He was fifteen and they were in their twenties. They even took our bus fare money.

Soon after that happened my mother made a remark to me about starting my period. I didn't know that she kept track of my periods. My friend Beth was staying with us because her dad was on a "drunk," according to her mother. What a coincidence: we were both pregnant at the same time and ended up having our babies, both boys, six days apart! Beth got pregnant from the rape in the front seat of that car and I wasn't sure when I got pregnant. So, I didn't know if I was going to have a black baby or a white baby. I could have gotten pregnant by my friend Leo or my friend Wally.

My parents, well, my mother thought the baby would be black because she answered the phone when it was for me and swore she could tell that the majority of my calls were from a "black boy." I denied it because it seemed to concern my mother, and I didn't want to "rock the boat." I never thought of it as being a problem; to me it was just my boyfriend calling me and nothing else.

In the summer of 1961, a friend of mine told me that a girl that I had only talked to once was no longer in school because she was pregnant. She had her baby, a boy, in August. She was only fourteen years old. When I received this information, I genuinely felt terribly sorry for her. None of her good friends stayed by her side once she got pregnant. I called her and asked if I could come to visit her and her baby, as I knew what it felt like to feel alone and uncertain of your future. So I went to visit Patty. Her baby was beautiful. After my visit, we became best friends and still are to this day. A year later on, I had my baby boy in July.

The summer after the ninth grade was without much drama. I saw Wally occasionally, and Leo the same. They both knew about each other, and they knew each other from school.

Chapter 3: My Three Sisters

After we moved into our middle-class neighborhood, all I remember of Arline was her and my dad fussing. They were so much alike. She was a penny pincher like my dad, which was good, as her family is very rich now. I found out when I was older that Arline had paid her own way to attend The Ohio State University.

Suzi and Kay got pregnant and had to get married. The unspoken words of the '50s and '60s (got pregnant); I too got pregnant at fifteen years of age but had no one to marry. We were, all four of us, baby-making machines. Arline had nine children, Suzi had three, Kay had three, and I had six. All of our marriages had problems, but Suzi's started and stayed bad.

Suzi was physically and mentally abused, as was her oldest son, whose dad ruined his life. She finally divorced her husband. He followed her to find out where she lived, just to harm her. She had to move three times in two weeks; my husband and I helped her. After a couple of years of living with my family, Suzi moved to an apartment where she thought her ex couldn't find her.

Suzi's ex-husband had threatened to kill himself for many years. On September 15, 1976, he found her and went to her apartment drunk and said he wanted to talk to her. She wouldn't open the door but told him to go home and call her, and she would talk to him on the phone. So he did, and while Suzi was talking to him on the phone, he said he couldn't live without her and was going to kill himself. She heard two shots and two groans, and he was dead. Suzi called the police and her ex-husband's brother.

The ex-husband's family blamed Suzi and her kids for his death. Everyone else knew it wasn't their fault, as he was an alcoholic and a womanizer.

Arline got a divorce and remarried. Kay got a divorce and remarried. Both sisters got good husbands with their second marriages. Both of their second husbands were decent and hard-working men, and they raised my sisters' children from their previous marriages as their own.

If you are abused by a boyfriend, or husband, or an inmate, there is help.

Please call The National Hotline for Abused Women, 1-800-799-7233.

Chapter 4: The Early 1960s

The early 1960s was a very chaotic time in our country. There was a lot of racial unrest. The only thing I knew about the Black people was the history of slavery and a saying that I heard quite often: "the races should not mix." I didn't understand why people said that. I was only fifteen and had been raised to love everyone. Our family was Christian, and I couldn't understand the double standard I was experiencing when I became pregnant. Now when I look back, I realize why my parents had felt the races shouldn't mix—because this is what they were taught.

Leo told me if I was having his baby, he would somehow find a way for us to be together and raise our child. His stated intent made me feel wanted and loved, but I knew down deep that dream could never happen. Besides our different skin colors, we were teenagers and still in school. Even though I honestly didn't know what love was, I could feel the love from Leo that I needed to hear and feel so desperately.

I was so confused and afraid when my mother said that if my baby was black, I would have to give it up for adoption for him to have a "normal" life. If the baby was white, I could keep the baby and they would help and support me. For seven months, my father wouldn't have anything to do with me, including not talking to me. Sadly, I couldn't tell who the father was because I didn't know myself. My friend Beth was also pregnant, and we made up a story that we were raped by some random hooligans. Beth and I thought this was a good cover story for our situation. Wrong again!

Our high school principal called Beth and me into his office and badgered us to tell him who the babies' fathers were. We stuck to our made-up story. Why did he want to know anyway? By the school rules, we were kicked out.

Beth's mother sent her to a Florence Crittenden home in Florida, so no one here would ever know she was pregnant and that she had to put her baby up for adoption.

I was given an in-home tutor. She was wonderful. She taught me more in six months than I had learned in ten years of school. She tutored me in every subject and was a former home economics teacher. I was taught to sew since, at that time, home economics was a choice in our subjects. I made all of my own maternity clothes, except for a few given to me by my older sisters.

During this time, initially, Wally acted excited about me being pregnant, then he took a deep breath and said, "I think I'm going to join the Navy." Both Wally and Leo knew that either one of them could be the father of my baby. While Leo stood by me as much as he could, Wally didn't speak to me again while I was pregnant. He even had a new girlfriend who lived a block away from me. When they would pass me on the street, Wally would act like he didn't know me. My pregnancy was not a happy one.

Chapter 5: Labor and Delivery

When I went into labor, my mother asked my father to drive us to the hospital because she was nervous. He said, "No, you will be fine taking her."

No one is allowed in your hospital room while you are in labor or delivery. I felt so alone and discarded. When I came out of the delivery room, I asked my mother who the baby looked like and she said Wally. I was glad but still disappointed. I got to keep my son but in a broken and loveless relationship. My son Bobby was born on July 25, 1962. As expected, my friend Beth's biracial son was born six days earlier on July 19th. Beth was only allowed to hold him once before his adoption.

A week after my son was born, Beth's mother called me and asked if I had given birth yet. I told her yes and that I named him Robert Allen and gave him my last name. She asked me if I had kept my baby. I told her yes. She said, "If I had known you were going to keep your baby, I would have let Beth keep hers too." That was a punch in my stomach. My and Beth's relationship was never the same after that.

I called Leo right away to tell him he was not my baby's father. Leo paused and then said, "I guess it is time for us to step out of our relationship so we both can go on with our lives." I cried and cried, but I knew he was right.

Chapter 6: On With my Life

I turned sixteen years old a month before Bobby was born. I also started summer night school, which was only during June and July. Because I had all As in my classes and had all my summer school subjects completed, I only had to go to summer school for one month (half the semester), and, in return, the school would drop my grades from all As to Bs. I needed July off to have my baby. I couldn't have cared less about grades because after my son Bobby was born, he was my number-one priority.

However, in the fall of 1962, I decided to go back to night school. My mother took care of Bobby while I was in class, but during the day I did all the care for him. Also, I was breastfeeding him, and several times at school, my breast milk would leak, and my shirt would get wet. I wondered if that turned my teacher on because of what happened next. One night when my shirt was wet, I was so embarrassed. My teacher wanted me to go on a date with him. I knew he was married, so I just shook my head. After all, I had never even been on a date, and for sure I wouldn't go out with a married man. Later on, that teacher became the principal at a local high school. I often wondered how many girls there he tried to date or worse.

I was clueless about my future. I graduated a year ahead of time, and I made the National Honor Society Roll. I was offered two or three scholarships. I declined them because all I was thinking about was loving and caring for my son Bobby and finding a good man to be his father. Besides, I had never thought about going to college. My mother told me girls would grow up, graduate high school, get married, and have children. I thought I had a more important mission to accomplish than getting more education.

Chapter 7: Family Life

I have never compromised my children's needs, whether it was financial, emotional, or anything for school or for sports. They came first before anybody else while they were growing up. It was my needs that I didn't recognize and act upon after years of turmoil, frustration, and loss of control of my son Bobby. I was always afraid of being told he was dead once he grew up because he was always in trouble. The only time I could relax was when he was in prison, and never in my dreams did I think I could find any peace before my children were incarcerated. It should have raised a red flag when Bobby was in the same prison as Alva. Alva was one of the inmates I met while I was working in the hospital. I became good friends with Alva because of the distance I felt from marriage; it felt good that I had someone who would listen to me. Bobby told me to be careful about my feelings and my relationship because every time he saw Alva, he had a lot of young men around him. Even though Alva had promised me he would make sure that Bobby was safe, Alva told me that murderers were the most respected inmates. Instead of questioning this information, I had tensions in the back of my mind. I was struggling with the thought that for Bobby to be safe, he might have to be one of those young men.

Mentally, I destroyed all that information so I could maintain some twisted balance for my future life. Bobby committed his first offense when he sold fake cocaine that was actually flour to an undercover police officer. Soon after that, Bobby was always in and out of prison. When Bobby was eighteen years old, he was given a three- to fifteen-year sentence, and because he couldn't stay straight, he continued on parole for fifteen years.

Bobby was still on parole when he was sent home. He was straight and OK at first, but it only took a couple of days to regain his only friend, heroin. Understandably, the other children were deeply affected by Bobby's addiction. I remember, one evening my kids and I were in the living room watching television. Bobby was in another world and kept putting the light of a flashlight on and off in everyone's face. David, one of my other sons, asked him to quit, and Bobby wouldn't. David was tired of all the drama and disruption that Bobby had caused our family, so David snapped. He got up and punched Bobby in the face, breaking a bone under his eye. Bobby had to go to the hospital. The whole situation broke my heart. Bobby couldn't fight back because he was stoned, and David had every right to express his feelings. My fourth son, Danny, was so upset that he punched the wall four times in quick succession and then ran out, going to the neighbors, crying all the while. Earlier on in the evening, the mood in the house was a gripping tension, as it was before this incident.

Chapter 8: My First Husband Jace

Jace, my first husband, was adopted when he was five years old. His adoptive parents had wanted to adopt a baby, but when they walked by Jace, he started to sing "Jesus Loves Me." Jace was not able to remember anything about the first five years of his life. He just knew he wanted a home. He was so cute that the couple decided to adopt him. Right away, Jace became a little rebel, and probably partly because they soon adopted a little girl. She got all of their attention and love. Jace got none. Jace said his parents were cold to him and told him they didn't love him. I believed him, but now I know it was because he was so rebellious. Jace told me his parents were always causing problems for him. I believed him at the time and figured they were trying to control his future.

Jace told me his parents had been missionaries. He said his father had a

Doctor of Divinity degree and was a minister of the third largest Methodist church in Ohio.

Jace's mother was on the board for the Methodist Children's Home, as well as a mother and a minister's wife. She led a very busy life. Jace's mother was very educated and made me feel very comfortable. She accepted my first child as if he was her very own

While attending night school, I met a cute young man named Jace. We started talking. He had a bubbly personality. The more we talked, I realized that I had met a talented, smart, and loving man. When Jace met my baby son Bobby, he was very loving and warm to him. My parents liked Jace at first, as he could sing and play the piano, and they liked the way he treated Bobby. We were all impressed with him.

Probably to make me happy or impress me, Jace told me he wanted to adopt Bobby. I told him he would have to ask Bobby's father, Wally, if it was OK with him. Without hesitation, Wally said he didn't care. I was very hurt, but I also felt relief knowing that my son would have a father now. I found out what Jace had to do. He just had to go to the courthouse and declare paternity, since there was no father's name on the birth certificate. The original birth certificate just had Robert Allen and my last name. It didn't really make any difference anyway because Jace never supported any of our sons.

I talked my parents into letting me marry Jace. I never thought about the downside of getting married at sixteen years old while Jace was eighteen. I already had one baby and was marrying someone I didn't love. Jace wanted to have sex before we were married. I said no, not until I got an engagement ring. Soon after that, I got my bubblegum ring, so when we got married, I was two months pregnant. When I met Jace's mother, she was very nice to me. She told me a few things about Jace and said she would tell me some more about him later, but she never did. I didn't want to hear anything else about him anyway. After all, I was getting a father for my baby. Both of his parents seemed loving, nice, and very accepting of my son Bobby.

Jace and I were married in my parents' home and lived there for a short while.

I should have listened to Jace's mother. On our wedding night, I woke up in a puddle of urine. Perhaps that was something Jace's mother wanted to tell me later.

Soon after we were married Jace did an about-face. He became mentally and physically abusive. On our second night of marriage, he wanted to argue with me over nothing. When I wouldn't argue, he got mad and pushed me hard when I was walking up the stairs. His demeanor and personality changed from sweet and loving to evil and abusive. My parents were shocked and upset.

One Sunday afternoon, the whole family went out. Jace went home before us and broke into the house. He stole some money from my parents' bedroom. Of course, he denied it.

I thought if we moved out, Jace would be better because my parents wouldn't be around to judge him. I also thought he might be showing off to let my parents know he was my boss. They begged me not to move out, but if I did would I please leave Bobby there with them. I couldn't leave him there, although he would have been better off.

I discovered that Jace was unfaithful to me. I had already graduated from high school by attending night school. Jace hadn't graduated yet, so he rode to night school with my mother, who was taking a typing class. One night I found Jace's wet underwear hanging on the shower rod to dry. When I asked him about it, he told me he had met a girl at night school and they went out to my mother's car and had sex in the back seat. The blood in his shorts was because she was on her period. Jace cried and promised he would never, never do that again. That was so disrespectful to my mother and me. I didn't tell my mother for a few years.

Jace and I eventually moved to a bigger apartment. Over the next two years, We both experienced a lot of changes in our lives. As far as my life-changing events, it's hard for me to look back and remember that I had a lot of bad things happening to me. I didn't know how to react to them. A few good things happened, too, and I've never felt bad about them.

It was November 1963. I was in bed for a nap when I heard something horrible on the radio. President Kennedy had been shot. He was in a motorcade in Texas with his wife, Jackie, and the Governor of Texas and his wife. No one else was hurt. The President was rushed to the hospital but soon died. The whole nation was in shock and disbelief.

About that same time, my water broke. I called my doctor and he told me to go to the hospital right away. I called my dad and he dropped me off on his way to work. When I got to the delivery floor, it was surreally quiet and empty. I didn't see any staff around. Finally, a doctor (probably an intern) came into my room to examine me. He said everything was fine, and I would be starting labor any minute because I was fully dilated. He told me the staff were all in the back watching the breaking news about Kennedy and Oswald. The doctor said someone would check on me a little later. This was on a Friday, so I wasn't allowed to eat for three days. On Monday, I was still leaking water and that meant I would have a dry birth, which is very serious and dangerous. My mother called my doctor and he was furious. He demanded that a resident start a Pitocin drip and to stay with me until I went to the delivery room. It only took one hour, and I finally had my baby, David.

Jace was getting harder to live with. He started to drink a lot. Then I found out he was seeing another girl he met at night school. When I questioned him, he was defensive. Jace said they had been seeing each other for a while and they had a baby girl. That really hurt me, as I had always wanted a girl. Jace told me his girlfriend's parents and family had only been in Columbus for a month or two and that her father was in the Army. They moved here from West Virginia. I found out later that Jace was not the baby's father. The baby's real father was in the Service and had been shipped out.

Now, he told me he wanted a divorce, and that he was going to move out. I had never spent a night alone. I had never worked or had any kind of training. I had to go on public assistance. So, I was scared and had high anxiety. I was so hurt and scared, so I begged him to stay, and I promised him I would do anything he wanted, that I would be his slave. I even blocked the door. So, I became his slave, and I was a fool who didn't know that Jace had stripped me of my identity and self-worth. He told me he didn't love me anymore and said again that he wanted a divorce. I told Jace's parents some of what was going on, without telling them all the details. Jace's father talked to Jace and told him he should stay with me and the kids until I had my fourth baby (by this time, we'd had a third baby already). Yes, I was pregnant again. Jace said he would stay and support us with his unemployment check until I had the baby, and then he would leave.

Jace made me feel so inadequate and afraid. He quit showing love for the kids over the last year and completely ignored them. He was a tyrant and tried to start arguments, but I wouldn't argue. The children were all still little, ages one to three years old, but when I looked at their tiny faces, I could tell they knew something was wrong. Jace called me names and kicked me in the stomach when I was five months pregnant. Jace was still lying and pretending to be going to night school. Every evening, before he would leave, he would gather up his schoolbooks. I assumed he was meeting his girlfriend or drinking because when he got home from "school," I could tell he had been drinking heavily. For one thing, the smell of liquor was on his breath.

Before I finish this chapter of my life, I want to go in to some behind-the-scenes activities. Since the beginning of our marriage, even after intercourse, Jace would go in the bathroom and masturbate. I felt I wasn't worthy or not enough for him. Growing up, I was always told I was a cute girl and very smart. They must have meant book-smart. I sure wasn't street-smart.

At this time in my life, I was very scared, hurt, and confused. I thought something was wrong with me. I just wanted to be loved. I didn't have anyone I could talk to, not even my parents.

Once, when I was eighteen, Jace came home from the store. A few minutes later, two detectives came to our door, and Jace explained that they were investigating a car wreck that he had witnessed. He left with the detectives and about an hour later, the sheriff called and said I would need money to bail Jace out of jail. He was arrested for masturbating in front of two fourteen-year-old girls. His punishment was for the two of us to talk to a counselor.

While at the counselor, Jace sounded like he had terrible hidden feelings about Bobby. The counselor said Jace felt some animosity toward Bobby. I asked the counselor if I should tell Bobby that Jace was not his biological father. He said no because his real father didn't want him and had no desire to become part of Bobby's life. I guess I agreed, or at least I understood what the counselor was saying. That was all we talked about; nothing was said about Jace exposing himself. Of course, Jace promised me he would never do anything like that again.

Another time that year, I found Jace ready to molest a preteen family member. I caught him just in time. I questioned him over and over, and finally, he admitted to liking young girls—as young as babies! He further told me that while he was babysitting at his father's church, he started molesting the children and even the babies. I am the only one he ever told. I had no idea who to tell or what to say. At that time, I made sure Jace wasn't around any young girls the best I could. I prayed he was never with his girlfriend's baby. Luckily, her mother babysat when Jace and his girlfriend would do their thing.

Have you ever thought you could "change" the person you were married to? Like, change him from engaging in bad behavior and everything associated with it to a good Christian mate who loved their family and lived a good clean life? Even a pedophile? I was so miserable that I even thought I wouldn't make it. Before I had begged Jace not to go, but now I wanted him to leave. Even though I was pregnant and had no way to support myself and my boys, I couldn't stand to be around him anymore. He had been laid off, so I knew he would use that as an excuse to stop supporting us. When I asked him if he would financially support us, he got really mad, and that's when he kicked me in the stomach.

On the last day of March in 1966, I was hurt and mad at the same time. I was tired of Jace's lies, his disrespect, his conduct, and his hate for our family. He was constantly saying he hated me, so then why had he wanted to marry me? He kept calling me a whore and saying that he knew when he moved out again, I would have a line of men waiting to come in and screw me. I had never given him a reason to think this unless he was referring to me having a baby out of wedlock. I never argued with him. In fact, I cried all the time after he first moved out.

Suddenly I realized that I felt some strength and felt strong enough to tell Jace I wanted him to move out right now, even though I was six months pregnant. What good was he for me and the boys? No matter, I was going to tell him we didn't need him anymore. On April 1, 1966, I watched the parking lot from a bedroom window to see when he got home to get my courage up to tell him he didn't need to stay here anymore, that he was free to go now. When Jace came through the front door, I got in bed because I could smell alcohol, and I was afraid of him when he was drunk. I thought it would be better to wait until morning. But I was too mad, and I had to say something. After he quietly got in bed, I said, "If you're not going to school, don't take your books like you are. You're a pig." Those were probably the most negative words I had ever said to him. He was quiet, and I didn't say any more. Normally, he would get mad and want to argue or say something mean or threaten me. I was surprised.

Around 10 a.m. the next day, I was lying on the bed resting for a few minutes. I was listening to some music on my radio. The music stopped, and a voice said "We have breaking news. During the night someone shot the driver of a car next to them." I thought that was terrible and couldn't fathom anyone doing that to someone else. The last words said about the shooting was that the woman identified the person who shot her. She said the person was a white man in a black car with a lot of primer on it that looked like tan colors in random circles. I suddenly got a sick feeling in my stomach. Someone just described my and Jace's car. Evidently, the car was spotted at a gas station across the street from the factory where Jace worked. At that time, he had been called back to work. The gas station attendant recognized the car from the news and called the police.

Jace was arrested and charged with shooting with intent to kill. The woman he shot was blinded in one of her eyes. She was a nurse who just got off work from The Ohio State University Hospital on campus. Ironically, years later, I worked at OSU Hospital East for ten years as a registered nurse before I retired. Later, when Jace was in prison, I learned that, originally, Jace was coming home to shoot Bobby and me. I never knew Jace kept a gun in the glove compartment of our car.

So now, at this point in my life, I was almost twenty years old, and I was six months pregnant with three small sons. My husband Jace and the father of my children was in jail waiting to be sentenced. He was sentenced to three to fifteen years in prison, but he only served three years.

I was twenty years old and had my four sons to take care of and support. I had Bobby, sixteen months old, born on July 25,1962; David, born on November 25, 1963; Timmy, born on March 25, 1965; and I had Danny, born on July 12, 1966, three weeks after my 20th birthday—all born sixteen months apart! I loved them all so very much.

I had to go on welfare since I had no working skills, and there was no way I could pay a babysitter so I could go to work, or when I visited Jace in prison. So, I took all the boys with me to visit him. He would give the boys a hug and say hi, and he would say, "How are you guys doing?" Then he would spend the rest of the visit wanting to talk to me about sex. Bobby went to the bathroom, which was for inmates and visitors, and when he took longer than Jace thought he should have, Jace went in to check on Bobby. When they came out, Bobby said Jace had said some very inappropriate things to him. It was then I finally said to myself, it's time to get a divorce, and I did.

As I sit here writing, I feel like I need to condense what I'm writing about each of my children, but sometimes I get tired of writing, tired of thinking, and I'm tired of remembering. The boys only heard from their dad, Jace, one time from a phone call. Danny, Bobby, and Timmy talked to him. David said he would only talk to him if he sent him some money. Of course, he never sent me any support money.

After my divorce from Jace, I met a man named A.J. through a friend of mine. We dated for a while. It was nice to get some good attention for a change. When we went out, I had to drink 3.2 beer. Back in the day, if you weren't twenty-one, the alcohol content could be no higher than 3.2 percent.

Then, I found out he was married. I cared a lot for him, and even though he hadn't met my boys, he gave me enough money to buy them Christmas presents. I genuinely appreciated him for doing that, but later I decided that was all he could give me of his life. So, I broke up with him. I moved to another location in the city so it would be easier for me to say no to him when he called and wanted to meet. After that, I met my second husband, Eddie.

Chapter 9: My Second Husband Eddie

In 1968, I met my second husband Eddie at a bar. I went out with a girlfriend that night. Eddie was sixteen years old, and I was twenty-two years old. I thought he was older, at least eighteen or nineteen, and I looked a lot younger for my age. We hit it off right away. We both liked to dance, and we liked to listen to the same music.

We dated for a few months. When Eddie met my boys, he liked them right away. We loved each other and decided to get married. One weekend soon after, we dropped one of the boys off at my parents' house and the other three at my friend Beth's. We eloped to Virginia with another couple who were friends of Eddie's. His friends had eloped there a month before and said it was a lot of fun. They said they would show us where we should go and what to do. I didn't tell my parents anything until I got back. Of course, they were upset, but as time went on, they got to love Eddie like a son.

Eddie would do anything for them. They thought he was eighteen years old, too, because that's what I told them. I didn't find out he was only sixteen until a few months later.

In 1969, I got pregnant right away with my and Eddie's first baby. I had a girl named Tracena. I couldn't believe it because I'd wanted a daughter for so long, and the doctor told me to turn my head and look. She was lying in an incubator beside my bed. I finally got my girl, but I wouldn't have taken anything for my boys. In between Tracena and my last baby, Eddie Joe, I suffered a miscarriage. It was hurtful and very sad for me, but Eddie took it even harder than I did. That was the first and last time I saw him cry. I told him I wanted to try one more time to have another girl. He finally agreed. So, three years after Tracena was born, Eddie and I had another baby, a boy named Eddie Joe. We decided six children would be enough for us to raise. My doctor told me I should have my tubes tied, so I did.

Eddie raised my boys as if they were his own, and the boys felt as though Eddie was their real father. They even took his last name.

Eddie loved my four oldest boys and treated them incredibly well. He coached their football and basketball teams. All the area kids wanted to play on Eddie's teams; their parents also wanted their kids to play for Eddie. He was highly respected. He was knowledgeable, kind, had a love for working and teaching kids in sports, and so his teams always won.

While Jace was still in prison, some other inmates and he started a theater group. When they were released, the inmates went around different cities and put on a play called "The Cage." Eddie heard they were going to be performing in Columbus, and he wanted us to go.

I was having my period and didn't want to go; also, I thought there might be a fight. I went anyway and sat in the back by myself. Eddie sat in the front row. When the play was over, Jace came back on stage and asked the audience if they had any questions. Eddie spoke up and said he had a question. He asked, "What do you think about a man that gets a divorce but doesn't pay any child support?" Jace hesitated and then said, "Everyone, this is my ex-wife's husband," and left it at that.

Eddie and I had been married for fourteen years when he started seeing this other woman. Evidently, I hadn't been the "perfect" wife and mother. We had some friends who lived a couple of blocks away, and Eddie went there almost every night. He met their sister while he was there one night and, later on, married her. After we separated, we still lived together because of the money problems we had. With me in school and having to pay tuition, everything was very tight financially. Eddie still lived at home, but we slept in separate beds. Even though I didn't want to be with him, it was easier to pay the bills with both of us contributing.

Although Eddie had a good job working at a trucking company, it took everything he made to support our family.

Back to my going to nursing school. I was thirty-two years old when I started nursing school. I had six children, ages three to fourteen years old. The oldest boy, Bobby, tried drugs and got addicted. My other children did not take that route. I took Bobby to a counselor. She thought going to college and then getting a job would help me deal with my addicted son and also build up my self-esteem.

She asked Eddie if he would be willing to help take care of the kids and help with the housework, and he said yes. Wrong again! It was difficult for me to carry this load, although Eddie thought I was not carrying my share of the load. However, Eddie was a very good father.

We had to find a way to pay for my college. Eddie helped me pay for college because we were still married and he was willing to still provide for me, even though we weren't on the best of terms at the time. Eddie loved to box and had a few matches where he would be able to win money. Eddie boxed under the name of "Rocky." So, he got back into the boxing ring and made enough money for my college. I graduated in 1984 and got a job at St. Anthony's Hospital. Since then, OSU bought it and renamed it OSU East.

The last two years of our marriage, Eddie was always putting me down and verbally abusing me. He also told me that when we first met, I was really sweet, and now, since I started school, I was a bitch.

Unknowingly I was sinking deeper and deeper into depression and felt like I had no one to confide in. On top of the depression I felt from my failing marriage, my oldest son started abusing drugs. Eddie wasn't Bobby's biological father, but he was always there for him. But during this challenging time, we had different ways of dealing with my son. We couldn't see eye to eye. He wanted to kick Bobby out in the streets. As his mother, I didn't feel comfortable kicking my fifteen-year-old child out. Eddie started going out of the house more and leaving me alone with the kids more than he had in the past. We ended up going to counseling to work on our marriage. We stayed together for one year afterward, but ultimately, after fourteen years of marriage, we made a mutual agreement to divorce.

After Eddie and I divorced, he married someone else right away. Even though no one cared what I thought, I didn't like her. She was mean to our children, so their relationship didn't last. Meanwhile, I was steady in my nursing career and in taking care of the kids. After years of us being divorced, I was still invited to his family get-togethers, since we all got along. They always celebrated the holidays and birthdays together. Eddie had been living with his girlfriend Louise, who was such a great woman. My kids and I were at their house for a family get-together. When we were getting ready to leave, Louise would always joke around saying

"take Eddie with you." We thought it was funny, and we all laughed about it. It became my and Louise's running joke, even though things ended "rocky"—pun intended. I finally had peace of mind with the ending of that chapter.

Chapter 10: My Third Husband Alva

After my first year working nights, my divorce was final, and my oldest son, Bobby, was going to prison because of drugs. While working the night shift, I had up to thirty-two patients at a time, and most were in critical condition. I only had one nursing assistant to help. A big percentage of the patients were very sick and unable to talk, which in itself is a hard condition to work in. There was one patient who was friendly and enjoyed talking, so when I was caught up with my work, I'd stop in his room to talk. The problem was, this likable gentleman was a prisoner, shackled to the bed with two armed guards. The patient himself told me he was incarcerated for murder, had served ten years, and was to be released in a couple more. Alva told me he saw a man harming a young girl, so he attacked him and killed him. Knowing that he had committed murder was a little off-putting, but for some reason, I convinced myself that what he did was honorable. I thought to myself: if it were my daughter I would've wanted someone to protect her. My loneliness and my vulnerability made me think: Well, what he did is not that bad. Due to my insecurities and experiences, I felt safe with him. He couldn't cheat on me because he was incarcerated. Most importantly, I felt wanted. Sometimes I would think: Who wants to be with someone who has six kids? And here Alva was, wanting to be with me. My head was in the clouds.

Alva was in the hospital for three weeks after having foot surgery, so by the time he left to go back to prison, I felt I had a new friend, and we started corresponding. He wrote daily, and the letters were beautifully written. He told me he had taken two college courses and that he received two degrees while in prison. He seemed quite intelligent. When I met Alva, he was an honorable inmate, and I witnessed a lot of respect for him from the chaplain, the staff, etc. First, the inmates want to exchange letters. Next, they want to call you and talk on the phone, which you have to pay for as they can only call collect. Then they want money and food boxes. These days there are no longer food boxes, so they want money so they can buy food in the prison. They also want money for name-brand tennis shoes. Did I fall for all these ploys? Yes, I did.

When Alva wrote me letters from prison, they started out like this: "My Darling, My Butterfly, My Wife, My Beloved Flower, My Beautiful Flower of Sweetness, and Precious Love." Later, they started with "Dear Sharol." It was another red flag that I didn't want to recognize. We had nicknames for each other. His was Renegade and mine was Butterfly.

Life was unbearable at times. I wanted a whole family, but one vital member was missing. I was continually questioning myself as to why I was willing to put my life on hold for this man. I would appease myself by thinking there must be reasons for me doing this and putting my kids through this too. I was spending years waiting for the release of a man who had committed a murder. Did I think so little of myself that I would take the risk of loving a felon and everything that goes along with it? I was a fool and didn't realize it until he got out of prison. Literally, when he was paroled, he walked out of the door of the prison, and I thought my dream was coming true. I thought he would grab me and kiss me, but it was quite the opposite. Alva didn't even touch me or allow me to touch him. His voice was stern as he said, "I don't want to be touched. Don't touch me!" Even when we were in the crowded visiting room in the prison, it sure wasn't hard for him to kiss me before and after a visit, so I found this behavior mystifying.

In almost all of Alva's letters, he said he didn't want anyone but me for the rest of our lives. When we got home, it was a different story. Alva was a different man than the one writing me every day while he was in prison. This wasn't the same man who told me over and over how much he loved me and that I was the only woman he would ever love and need, etc.

Alva told me so many lies. It seems like it was a million years ago now. The things I was learning and observing were that I wasn't what Alva wanted. My house was not good enough, my kids were taking advantage of me, and I didn't have enough money to suit him. After all I had done for him, including buying him new clothes and shoes and anything else he wanted, nothing about me was good enough for him. He should have been on his knees, thanking God for me. Instead, he moved out in six weeks. I was totally devastated and demoralized.

There was another incident when he was still in jail where an inmate was beating up a female guard. Alva grabbed the inmate and held him down until other guards could get there. He was given credit for saving the female guard's life. Only good things were told to me when the prison social worker and the prison chaplain sat down at our table with us. They also told me about his college endeavors and receiving his associate degree. I was very impressed with all of that positive information. This information contributed to the feeling I've processed about Alva making parole and living the dream life together. Holidays were especially lonely and depressing for me. Even though my family always got together during the holidays, it made me feel incomplete because Alva wasn't there with me. My kids knew how I felt, and they tried everything they could to make me happy. I was being selfish but didn't know it, or I didn't want to know it. I was emotional, and I just wanted to be with Alva (or who I'd built him up to be).

I cried a lot, especially on my way home after a visit with Alva. I can still hear the words of this song on my car radio forever: Neil Diamond singing "September Morn."

Wow! I didn't get to start living my dream after all. Instead, I started living a nightmare. I am sure all the people who were telling me it wasn't good to fall in love with a prisoner were now thinking in their heads, I told you so. I really didn't care what anybody was thinking. All I could think about was the life I wanted to share with him.

I worked very hard to help Alva get his parole. I wrote letters to public officials, and I talked to the Parole Board on his behalf. I also made a lot of phone calls and did a lot of running around to get Alva and myself a marriage license. And I had to get permission from the Warden to get married in prison. My sister Suzi tried to talk me out of it, but I wouldn't listen to her. Suzi said if that was what I truly wanted, she would support me. So, I had a prison wedding. Not very romantic, huh?

Alva was in prison for twenty years for murdering someone during an armed robbery in 1972. Now remember, he told me he murdered someone to save a little girl. It was all a lie! I didn't find out a lot about his past until he was sentenced for murdering an eighteen-year-old boy and stealing his truck.

Alva was on parole for five years, but never finished it. It is a shock that

Alva shackled himself, and he became his own worst enemy. He progressed from armed robberies to murder. I feel a lot of guilt since I worked so hard to get him released, and then he ended up committing another murder. I have also worked hard to get rid of my guilt, but it's hard when an eighteen-year-old boy is shot twice in the back of his head after begging Alva not to hurt him. Alva told him that he wouldn't hurt him and then shot him.

Years later, Bobby was still addicted to drugs. He ended up getting caught with drugs on him, which was a parole violation. He was sentenced to three to fifteen years in prison. He was sent to the same prison as Alva. Bobby told me to be careful because he found out some things about Alva that I should know. One of the things was that Alva liked young boys. A red flag that I ignored. I ignored it because I would have had to accept that my prince charming was actually a prince from hell, and I wasn't ready to do that.

During this time, I started taking EMT classes, and I was still working at the hospital. My daughter had a baby boy, born on Alva's birthday. I took my grandson to visit Alva. When Alva saw him, he just beamed and sometimes held him throughout the whole visit. He said if I was at work that he would be glad to babysit. I felt happy because it sounded like soon all my dreams would be coming true when he made parole. Little did I know that one of the first things he said to my daughter when he got out was that she needed to get her son and herself out and take care of them on her own. It raised yet another red flag considering, since he was talking very angrily. That was the opposite of what he said in prison. He had suddenly changed his attitude and demeanor.

My best friend was a friend of a parole officer who tried in every way to discourage me from marrying Alva, but to just stay with him. Of course, I didn't listen.

Alva and I often got into arguments about him not meeting my parents. But, if I'm being honest, I just wasn't comfortable with him meeting them. Deep down inside, I'm sure I knew something wasn't right with him. My parents were older by this point, and I didn't want to disappoint them. They knew nothing of my relationship with him, and I felt like this would send them over the edge. After an intense disagreement, Alva finally agreed to meet them. He kept telling me I was embarrassed of him and, truth be told, I was. I prayed the entire day that he would be on his best behavior. That evening I took Alva to my parents' house so they could meet one another. Everything was going so well at first. I thought to myself, I should've done this sooner. But as soon as the thought came to my mind, it immediately left because Alva told my dad he had a job, but he needed a car to get to work. He asked my dad for a loan, and Alva said he would pay him back a certain amount of money each week. My dad loaned Alva the money for a used car, and I kind of wish he hadn't. As soon as Alva got the car, he started acting differently toward me. He felt as though he could get up and go and not talk to me about anything. The crazy part of this all is he didn't even have the car for a week before he told me he would be moving out. I was confused because I still had hopes of us building a life together. But he had other plans. He told me that he needed to be more independent, and the best way to do that would be to move out. He never paid my dad back his money, and I felt horrible. But I still hoped that things would get better.

I got Alva a job at an alcohol rehab center through a friend of mine. I felt bad asking her, but we needed money, and he needed a job. I was hoping this job would work out, but he got fired for going to work drunk. How could you go to work drunk when working for a rehab facility? Again, I felt the same embarrassment and shame I felt when he didn't pay my dad the money back. After he was fired, I found out he met a woman in rehab and moved in with her and her young son. He really left me for another woman after everything I did for him. It's like he just wanted to hurt me intentionally. Alva told me, bragging, that he was able to have sex with her. Our marriage was never consummated. So, this really hurt me deeply. That was Alva's way of punishing me, but I don't know why. There was no physical touching, even though he asked one of my teenage boys if he could get him a prostitute. Ten years of my life just became a failure, a loss of love and intimacy. It made me feel very unappreciated, undervalued, and most of all, I felt like a fool.

Later, Alva came to my job to borrow money and said he needed a place to live. I told him my own son was homeless, so why would I give him a place to live and not my son.

Alva was on parole for five years. Three months into his parole he was committing armed robberies. During one of these robberies, he was in a gunfight with the carryout owner and the police. A bullet grazed Alva's head. While in the hospital, he told everyone his legs were paralyzed. He returned to prison in a wheelchair and feigned paralysis for months. When it was time for him to go to court, a female guard did not shackle him because she thought he was paralyzed. Evidently, the doctor at the prison was not totally convinced Alva was paralyzed but did not pass that information on to the prison staff. Alva stayed in the wheelchair.

As the guard was wheeling Alva in the parking garage at the courthouse, he grabbed the officer's gun and pistol whipped her and ran out of the parking garage. Alva saw a young man getting in his truck and highjacked the man and his truck. The man was an eighteen-year-old boy who just had paid his parking ticket and was on his way to his grandma's house for dinner. He begged not to be hurt, and Alva promised he wouldn't hurt him. Alva made the boy take off his shirt and give it to him. He then shot the boy in the head, execution style. That boy trusted Alva, just as I had done for ten years.

Instead of driving to get out of town, Alva drove through two beer drive-throughs to buy forty-ounce beers. He drove to a shopping center and tried to hijack another car. He was unsuccessful, but then he did get a second car.

I was at work and in a patient's room. Breaking news came on the TV with live coverage of the escape of a convict from prison. Alva was found hiding in a tree, and the police had him surrounded. The patient I was with said, "Hey, that's my house and my tree!" I was thinking to myself, Yeah, and that's my ex-husband. Alva was charged with first-degree murder and sentenced to the death penalty. Alva also had a lot of other convictions before all of this happened. I received a letter from him after his incarceration, but I did not answer it.

My marriage to Alva lasted three years. We got married in 1990 while he was still incarcerated, and he was released in 1992. The divorce was finalized in 1993. We only lasted one year outside prison. It wasn't a real marriage. We had no intimacy, no communication, and we didn't have love. Our marriage was never consummated. I never got my fairytale ending with Alva. But everything I went through with him changed me for the better. I learned a lot in those three years. My trust was completely broken when it came to men.

Women! Please don't fall for these lies. I have a life-changing story that I'm sharing in the hope it will help at least one person, hopefully more, from suffering the hell of a bad decision made with good intentions.

Chapter 11: My Fourth Husband Kelly

I met Kelly in the summer of 1993, when he was a patient at the hospital. I wasn't looking for love, but I wanted someone to talk to, and we had good conversations. He was a window washer, and while doing his job one day, the scaffolding broke and he fell. The fall broke his back.

We fell in love and got married on May 13, 1997, my parents' wedding anniversary. First, we moved into an apartment until I could get my house sold and buy another one. My son E.J. was in college in Pennsylvania and came home on the weekends. I told him he could stay with us, but when he left the next morning and hadn't made his bed, Kelly said he could not stay there anymore. That should have been another red flag, but I didn't recognize it. Looking back, I can't believe that I was willing to risk the relationship with my son for a man because I was scared to be alone. I thought we were in love, but I had married a high-maintenance person. Kelly wasn't able to work due to his back injury. So I paid the house payment and all the bills. Most nights he would leave, telling me he had a friend who owned a carryout, and he was supposedly going to help him stock his shelves. I knew it was B.S., but I just wanted to make this work; this was my fourth marriage.

At one point in our marriage, my oldest son Bobby needed a place to live temporarily. He was drug-free at that time, but Kelly said he wasn't allowed in our home, and I shouldn't let him come if he was high. I told Kelly that Bobby was not on drugs now and that he was my son, and I would decide if he was allowed in my house or not.

The next thing I knew, Kelly let his son Kevin move in. Kevin's room was always a mess. His clothes were thrown everywhere. He left the lights on all night. He left the gate open at the top of the basement steps so the dog Sheba would eat all of the cat food continually. He never cleaned the cat litter. When he didn't come home at night, he never called to tell us. Of course, that was worrisome. He drove my car and wrecked it and never paid me back. When Kelly was sick and in the hospital toward the end of his life, Kevin drove Kelly's jeep and wrecked it too. He never showed any concern and never paid for it either. Kevin never took any responsibility for totaling his dad's jeep or even said he was sorry. He said he spent all of his paycheck on "car insurance." Kelly was dealing with his son's mess, and he didn't want my son here because he forgot to make up his bed! I felt foolish, but I was scared to be alone, even if that meant dealing with things that I didn't want to deal with.

As Kelly's cancer progressed, he eventually was under complete care. I had just had surgery in October 2001, so it was a lot for me to get back and forth from the hospital because I was recovering. Kelly had daughters and stepdaughters who never offered to help me. I tried to call them but got no response. Kevin lived with us but wasn't home much. When Kelly got worse, Kevin and a friend of his took Kelly to the E.R. The hospital admitted Kelly right away. That was November 2001.

I worked with a doctor who was Kelly's cancer doctor. The doctor and I talked about Kelly's condition. The doctor said he didn't have long to live. Kelly had told me before he got sick that he never wanted to be hooked up to machines. He didn't want to live that way. When he was dying, one of his daughters asked me about his code status. I told her what he had said, but she said it was my idea and not her dad's. His daughters blamed me for everything.

When Kelly was in the hospital dying, his daughter Terri was visiting him. She saw a newspaper lying there, open to a dating site. A nursing assistant had left it in the room on her 11 p.m. to 7 a.m. shift. Terri said something to me so her dad could hear her, as he was semiconscious but awake. She accused me of looking for a new man already. I was constantly being told I was killing him because I had a big insurance policy on him.

Kelly's daughter Donna needed a car. Since he didn't work, he wanted me to co-sign for her. I didn't want to, but he made me sign for her. While Kelly was healthy, Donna made her car payments. She also told her dad that I should pay her payments because I made more money than she did. When he got sick, she didn't make any more payments. I didn't know it at first, but then Beneficial Loan Company started calling me, and they were so rude. I told them to send the bill to me, and I would take care of it. I didn't want my credit to get ruined. I didn't hear from Toyota until the end of 2002. At that time, they told me they had repossessed the car. They said I had a choice to either buy the car back for $14,000 or ruin my credit and have a lien put on my house. I had no choice but to use the remaining $15,000 of Kelly's life insurance money. The other $12,000 paid for his funeral.

Two of my sons drove me to Canton Ohio during a blizzard to pick up the car. The windshield wipers' control arm was totally removed from the steering wheel column. We had to find a car repair shop to fix it and buy windshield wipers before we could drive home. Another hundred dollars was spent, besides what my sons lost in wages from taking the day off. The car had to be towed to Canton, and I also had to pay for that tow. Plus, they charged me the daily rate for the car sitting on their lot.

After five weeks had passed since Kelly died and I had experienced a few days of acceptance, I called Kelly's daughter Donna. She started yelling at me, asking me why I had her car repossessed. Donna told her whole family that I had it repossessed and, of course, that put more fuel on the fire. I was mad and hurt from this, along with all the accusations that I wanted him dead, wanted his insurance money, and was looking for a new man, etc.

Kelly passed away on December 10, 2001, from cancer. None of his kids would talk to me at the funeral home. They completely ignored me and my family. They wouldn't talk to me after the funeral at my home either. However, they did come to my home after the funeral to eat. Donna blew up at me. She said I didn't let them plan anything. Kelly's daughter Marcy shook her head in agreement. Kevin kept silent and didn't even stand up for me. Kelly's mother lost it because of their actions. We almost had to take her to the hospital. One comment was made that I should have used a "black" funeral home because "white" funeral homes don't know how to make up black people. They were wrong. Kelly looked so good and so handsome lying there.

Throughout this whole blurred time of my life, the only one of Kelly's kids who never turned against me and has stayed in touch with me to this day was Sally. She was only sixteen years old and a junior in high school. Sadly, five months earlier, she was the one who found her mother dead. She had died in her sleep from a heart condition. Sally was undoubtedly the most mature person and the most supportive of all of Kelly's children.

Chapter 12: My Children:

My First Son Bobby

I am starting out with the years from 2003 to 2006. This is my letter to my son Bobby. "It's been one year since you went home. You have no more fear, no pain, and you are never alone. Our family loves you and misses you. But now you are with your Heavenly Father. We are still earthly, and He is God with His unconditional love, and with our everlasting love, you are assured of your place in your Father's heavenly home. Wait for us and pray for us. Our Lord Jesus Christ gave the ultimate sacrifice for our sins. Some day we can once again all be together in the arms of our Lord."

My oldest son Bobby you already know something about. He was built, little, and short. He got bullied by other kids. His stepfather Eddie was the coach for the boys' football and basketball teams. Bobby loved all sports and was happy that his stepdad was his coach. When Bobby was fourteen, he was playing in a baseball game and got a hit. He ran, and he slid into second base. The shortstop said, "Way to go, shorty." That made Bobby mad, but he didn't respond. After the game, the two teams were supposed to shake hands. Instead of shaking hands with the guy that embarrassed him by in front of everyone, Bobby hit the guy in the face. As a result, Bobby was kicked out of the league. I think that started his downfall. He no longer had a buffer or release for all the teasing. When the boys became older, Eddie didn't coach them anymore.

When Bobby was fourteen years old, he began smoking weed. He probably felt invisible, as he was teased and taunted since he was six years old because he was considerably smaller and shorter than most boys his age. He was able to tolerate the bullying as long as he was able to feel good about himself from playing well on any given sports team he was on at that time. He soon became addicted to stronger drugs.

He had a lot of troubled years, a lot of ups and downs. Marijuana became his friend. Soon after, he was around the stoners most of the time. Most of his "friends" were experimenting with harder drugs, and Bobby followed along. Eddie and I were on opposite ends as to what we could do to end this horrible situation. Bobby's brothers didn't know how to handle the situation either because they were also just teenagers.

Our home was like a maze. We were all like zombies in a world we were not familiar with. No one was able to get any sleep, as we were never sure when Bobby would come home, and Eddie had to get up early for work. When Bobby did get home, if you happened to be asleep when he arrived, you would soon be awakened from hearing him humming and clanging the pots and pans and opening and closing the oven door to fix himself something to eat. I would have to go to the kitchen to make sure he wasn't about to set the house on fire. When he first saw me, he would lightly pinch my shoulder, smiling and calling me "Mummy." He acted like he didn't have a care in the world. I remember staying up all night by his bedside, making sure he was breathing. We never knew what condition Bobby would be in when he came home. It was a home of sadness, depression, and frustration. It was a never-ending saga.

Every day, when Bobby came home high, depending on his actions, we could tell what substance he had taken. On rare occasions, he came home and behaved aggressively and wanted to fight with his stepdad. It was so sad because before he started taking drugs, he and Eddie were very close. He thought of Eddie as his father, not his stepfather. Eddie wouldn't fight with him; he could only hold Bobby down until he calmed down. Several times, he wouldn't calm down, and we had to call the police to intervene so nobody would get seriously hurt. He regularly returned in the middle of the night. One time he came home, and once again wanted to fight Eddie. Eddie held him down after scuffling on the floor. Bobby tried to be calm. So, Eddie let him get up, and we thought Bobby was going to go to bed, but instead, he came back with a wine bottle and hit Eddie over the head, causing the bottle to break into a million little pieces. I called the police, and they took him downtown and put him in a holding cell with some other men. Bobby said, "What is this place, a bunch of Oreos?" Eddie wanted to hit him so badly but restrained himself—after all, Eddie was a winning Golden Gloves Boxer, weighing close to 195 pounds, and Bobby weighed about

110 pounds and was only five feet, four inches. So, if Eddie had hit Bobby, it would have been fatal.

There was such a damaged net over our whole shattered family that none of us could function normally or even feel some semblance of a connection with each other. Everyone loved Bobby as a kid, but not as an emerging man.

Eddie and I searched everywhere for help for Bobby and for the rest of our family. The best we could find were meetings with other parents with the same kind of concerns and problems. They were clueless too. When we went to a counselor, there were other people there with similar problems. We learned to take care of ourselves and our wants and needs, which helped us to better take care of our drug-addicted children.

Bobby was the only one of our children who did anything criminal, and he felt lost from our family. This was because of drugs, and he was always in and out of prison. Between two prison stints, after he returned home, he became incredibly religious. He said he gave his life to God and started reading the Bible. He loved and acted like the Bible fit right in with the new lifestyle that he was living. He talked a lot about God and he read the Bible so much that he knew the verses. Despite this, when he got home from prison, he went right back to the drugs. Bobby didn't work or apply himself to the needs of our family or even himself. I never had any doubt that he would go to Heaven when he died because he had learned about God, and he had repented.

When Bobby was forty years old, he started his own lawn care company, and for two years he was drug-free. In March of 2005, he wanted me to have a birthday party for his sister Tracena and his brother Timmy, because they were both born in March. A week later, on March 19, 2005, I had the party. Bobby never showed up.

The day before Bobby was found dead, he had been to the doctor and got some prescriptions. The pharmacy was not supposed to fill these prescriptions, according to his parole officer. They were supposed to put this order in his file so the pharmacy should have known not to fill these prescriptions. On Bobby's death certificate, it said drug overdose. The doctor I worked for had worked previously on the bloodwork from autopsies. He read the autopsy and the lab results. There was a very small amount of heroin in his system, but he tested positive for all the drugs that he had just gotten filled at the pharmacy the day before. The mixture of those medications with the heroin caused a spasm in his heart, which he died from. He did not die of a heroin overdose. Bobby was found on the floor like he was on his knees praying.

The next day, my son-in-law, Tracena's husband, came to my house with the bad news. He told me Bobby was dead from an overdose. Karma can be cruel. After two years clean, Bobby thought he could cheat death again. He had overdosed before but was revived. He had been renting a room at his biological father's house. Wally was the one who found Bobby. He always doubted he was Bobby's father, even though Bobby looked like him.

Bobby told me one time that all he ever wanted out of life was a wife, children, and to be a baseball coach. He loved kids and loved to coach Little League football. Bobby also coached a young boys' basketball team in our church gym.

It was very heartbreaking when Bobby died. I found some letters he had written and read them. He had written them to God, thanking Him and praising Him for never leaving him alone. Bobby always talked to and asked God for forgiveness for all the things that he put his family through. He also wrote individual letters to every family member that he was so very sorry for the things he did to cause all the hurt and heartache. He said he loved all of us, and he asked for our forgiveness. He had never thought he would turn into the man that he had become. He wanted to be able to coach football and basketball with young kids, and this did happen during the two years that he was straight before he died. RIP Bobby.

A lot of people are searching for answers. If you are living with an addicted person, today there is a lot more help.

If you need help or know of someone who needs help, please call: The National Hotline at 1-833-888-1553 or the Ohio Hotline at 1-877-275-6364.

My Second Son David

David was a good son and very smart in school. David found out he had a son when his son was twelve years old. His name was J.R. David and J.R. changed J.R.'s last name to Temple after David's last name. J.R.'s mother was married with another son. That son got all the attention from J.R.'s stepfather, and J.R. just caught heck. So, his mother sent him to live with his real father, David. He lived with David until he graduated from high school. When J.R. was old enough, he joined the Army. He served a little over three years. He served part of that time in Iraq. J.R. became addicted to drugs and was honorably discharged because of it. He wanted to get some help, so the Army got him counseling.

During this time, J.R. was married, and he and his wife Amber had two beautiful children: a boy named Nicholas and ,two years later, a girl named MacKenzie. I should have mentioned earlier that J.R. did well in school. He was very smart, and he was very good at sports. He especially loved playing baseball. He was a bowling champion with three 300 games (a perfect score). When J.R. was a senior in high school, he was offered two scholarships. One for bowling and one for baseball, but he turned both of them down. When J.R. got addicted to drugs, David gave him three options: go to college, get a job, or move out. He moved out.

J.R. then moved in and out of his maternal grandparents' house. They loved him very much and would do anything for him, including giving him money that he used for drugs. His grandparents might have felt some guilt because of the way their daughter treated him. Now their daughter was married again. David hadn't had the option to watch his children grow up, so he did everything he could for his grandkids. J.R. and his wife got a divorce, and she wouldn't let J.R. see the kids because he was on drugs. But she would let David see them and do things with them. David was involved in their sports and even bought their uniforms. He provided transportation back and forth and even paid for their out-of-town and out-of-state games. MacKenzie wanted to take lessons to learn how to ride horses. David bought those lessons for her, which were very expensive. He brought the kids to see me and also to see their great-grandma.

He would do anything to be close to them growing up. He was more like a father than a grandfather to those kids.

By now, J.R. looked and acted like he was on something stronger than weed. It wasn't hard for me to recognize a heroin user since my own son was a heroin user.

One time, when J.R. and his cousin Devan left a celebration at Eddie's house, they stopped at a drug dealer's house, but no one was there except the dealer's wife.

J.R. went back to the drug dealer's house later by himself. (From now on, I am going to call the drug dealer Master X.) He and his wife were at home, and his wife told Master X that J.R. had been there earlier and had stolen one of his guns. The man had about fifteen guns lying out on a large table at the time. I am thinking to myself that Master X was selling more than drugs. While accusing J.R. of stealing the gun, Master X and his friend jumped J.R. and began beating him, first in the house and then in the front yard. J.R. got away from them and ran to his car. Once he got to his car to take off, Master X started shooting at J.R. and managed to seriously wound him. J.R. was struck with five bullets, but somehow, he drove himself about three blocks to a gas station and then passed out.

While J.R. was in the hospital, his wife filed for divorce, which was understandable. The worst thing that happened concerning the divorce was that Amber decided J.R. was not allowed to see the kids anymore, not even with a supervised visit. She never told the kids anything good about their dad and made sure to tell them that he didn't want to be their father, which was a lie. Even when J.R. got off the drugs, Amber did not change her rule.

A few years ago, while Amber was on drugs, she wouldn't let David see her kids anymore either. J.R. hadn't seen his kids for eight or nine years, and he wanted Amber's phone number so he could talk to the kids. David didn't see any harm in that. So, David gave J.R. her phone number, and that made Amber mad. She didn't want J.R. to have her phone number or her address.

Amber told Nick and MacKenzie that their Grandpa David didn't care about them anymore, and that he didn't want to be around them or do anything for them. That really bothered David because they had become a big part of one another's lives. They all loved each other very much. No one in our family was ever allowed to see the kids, not even on holidays. Karma works in its own time. Amber and her mother got evicted for the fourth time and were both on drugs. That was when she called J.R. to take the kids. She asked him to pick them up and drop her off at a drug rehabilitation place. When J.R. picked them up and MacKenzie got in the car, her mother said, "Oh yeah, Kenzie, this is your dad," and Kenzie started crying uncontrollably.

J.R. is now drug-free, remarried, and has three stepchildren but still has room for his two kids. But since MacKenzie didn't remember her dad, the kids went to David's house first for a while. They met a few times to get acquainted and then went to live with their dad J.R. I don't know what will happen when Amber gets out of rehab. I can't imagine what it would be like now after all this time. Nick is seventeen and MacKenzie is fourteen. I hope everything goes well for Nick and MacKenzie. They are the ones I am really worried about.

David was laid off from a good job as a financial advisor of a big company at the beginning of the COVID-19 pandemic and is now trying to get caught up and better himself. He has a master's degree and is looking for a better job.

My Third Son Timmy

I was eighteen when Timmy was born. His birth was during the time when his dad Jace had started drinking heavily. He wasn't home much and really didn't act like he wanted to be a part of my pregnancy or my life. I remember begging him to help me with the other boys so we could take Timmy to get his first haircut. He told me I could handle all three boys by myself. He seemed so disconnected from me and the boys.

Timmy was a quiet baby, and even as he got older, he was like a little love bug. Timmy was bigger-boned than the other two boys, but he was as big as they were. Timmy wasn't at all aggressive. He wouldn't even defend himself when the older boys played rough with him or teased him. Most times, he would just come to me crying. He was also very good at sports. When he was around eighteen, he moved out to an apartment. He met and married a girl named Teresa. Eight months after they were married, Teresa had a baby boy they named Terry. In the next couple of years, they had a little girl named Devan. Their marriage didn't last long. After the divorce, Teresa moved back with the kids to Belfry, Ohio, where she had grown up. We didn't get to see the kids as much as we wanted. Besides the distance, Teresa soon got remarried and letting the kids see their dad was not a priority with her new husband.

Timmy had problems with his marriages, and he also had problems with his kids, Terry and Devan. When Terry was around seven years old, Teresa called Timmy and told him that she started going to church and it made her feel like she needed to tell Timmy the truth about Terry. She told him she had a one-night stand with a guy she had met at a bar. That was why Terry was born eight months after she and Timmy got married. We thought he was born early, but the doctor told us the baby was full-term. This was like a knife stabbing Timmy in the heart. He told Terry that, as far as he was concerned, he still considered Terry to be his son and he would always treat him as his own. Timmy continued to give Teresa child support for both of his children. Timmy was still the love bug, and he had a very big heart.

When Terry was just a teenager, he started using drugs. He was in and out of prison for his drug addiction. Every one of us tried to help him, but to no avail. Nothing worked, and now Terry is in what we call a "tough-love program." Our family tried to make Terry feel like a part of us, but he didn't appreciate it, so that's why everybody quit trying to help him. I still don't think our family has totally written him off. Devan is living in West Virginia and is recovering from drug addiction. She has partial custody of her daughter Maylene.

Soon after that, Timmy met a dancer, a stripper. She already had a little girl. Timmy and his new girlfriend got married and soon thereafter had a baby girl named Autumn. Even though she and her first daughter's dad left her and never returned, our family thought that was a really bad thing to happen to anybody. We had no way of knowing that this was a lie. We found out later that her older daughter's dad didn't want anything to do with Autumn's mother.

So, she did the same thing with Autumn. She convinced Autumn that her dad didn't care for her and didn't want her around. One day Timmy came home from work, and all the belongings of his wife and the girls were gone, and she left no message. Timmy had thought they had a good and solid marriage. He had no knowledge of why and where they had gone—not until he received an order from a Florida court telling him he had to pay $500 a month in child support. At that time, he had a good job working for the state, so he didn't object to the amount he was ordered to pay. Shortly after that, he lost his job and started working as a cook in miscellaneous restaurants for lower pay. It was too late to ask for a reduced child support payment. Timmy and his brother Danny moved into a trailer and still had problems paying their bills together. Timmy still didn't have an address or a phone number for his daughter Autumn. He hadn't seen her since she was eighteen months old, when her mother walked away from their marriage in Columbus, Ohio, and moved to Florida. Through Facebook, I was able to get Autumn's phone number, and we talked off and on through the years. When Autumn was eighteen, the child support payments stopped.

It is now 2023, and Autumn has her own baby girl that she named Sunny. The pictures of Sunny that Autumn posts on Facebook look exactly like her Grandpa Timmy when he was a baby. What a beautiful little girl. I can't wait to meet her.

Autumn was recently in the hospital. She was living with a boyfriend in his house. They broke up, and he told her to move out.

He then moved four hours away and moved in with his parents. He would come over to babysit for Sunny while Autumn was in the hospital. Before she returned home, he took Sunny and her belongings back with him to his parents' house. Prayers for Autumn and her baby Sunny. He had given Autumn a car at the beginning of their relationship. But when he took the baby, he also took her car keys so she couldn't come after Sunny. When he moved out, Autumn took care of their daughter by herself. It seemed as though he was using the baby to get back at her because she didn't move out of his house as soon as he wanted. It would have been easier to get an eviction notice. It was really a kidnapping because they had never gotten married or went to court for visitation rights. A week later she did get her baby back. She was selling her artwork in order to get a lawyer when he brought the baby back to her. Autumn was born in Florida and now lives in South Carolina.

Timmy had a third marriage, but it didn't last very long. It must have been a spur-of-the-moment thing. They were only together for a few months, and they separated and neither one of them got a divorce for several years, but finally, she got the divorce because she was ready to marry someone else.

Earlier this year I got a phone call from a girl named Emily. She told me she lives in Kansas and was told by her DNA test that it matched with Danny or Timmy Temple. A second cousin of mine was working on a family tree and found that Emily's DNA matches with two of my boys. Timmy had dated her mother, so we knew who she belonged to. He never even knew that his girlfriend had been pregnant and that she had a daughter and put her up for adoption.

Emily stated that she had great adoptive parents who she would like to meet all of us. Emily has three children. We would like to meet her too. I have talked to her on the phone a few times.

So, to break it down, Timmy has three daughters, one son, and seven grandchildren. Timmy's life is like a game of Monopoly.

Timmy is now a department manager for a large grocery chain.

My Fourth Son Danny

With my fourth son Danny, I got a weird feeling before and after he was born, just like the feeling I have now. Danny was born on July 12, 1966. A month earlier, I turned twenty, and three months earlier, my husband Jace shot a nurse on the freeway with a bullet that was meant for me and my older son Bobby. That happened on April 1, 1966. (I talked about this incident earlier.)

I was overwhelmed and scared about my future and the future of my kids. My dad wanted me to get a divorce after that happened, but I told him that I could only do that when I was ready. I felt some kind of an obligation to Jace, but now I realize that was very stupid and the only thing that should've been on my mind was how I was going to care for four boys under the age of four. I tried to keep everything under control by taking every problem as it happened. With Danny being my last baby, I needed to spend time with him. I wanted to be a good mother to him and my other boys. This was me answering my own question about the kind of mother I should be.

Luckily, Danny was a good quiet baby. I thought I deserved a baby girl after all I had been through. When I first saw Danny, he was so tiny and so beautiful, I knew things were exactly the way they were supposed to be. I felt so lucky to have a healthy baby boy as precious as he was.

When Danny started kindergarten, I picked him up on the first day. I asked him if he liked his teacher. He said, "Yes, I like her. She has freckles just like I do." He was so cute to say that, and he still has the freckles on his nose.

Danny was a good boy growing up. David and Danny were always teasing Timmy because he wouldn't stand up for himself. Danny particularly picked on Timmy because they were closer in age. One day Danny called me at work crying. He said Timmy punched him, and I asked what happened, and Danny told me that Timmy said he was tired of being teased. I was kind of laughing in my head, but I didn't let Danny know that. I was thinking: *Well, you had it coming*. Danny never retaliated, but he quit teasing Timmy.

When Danny was around twenty years old, he was at a wilderness ranch to learn how to work outdoors. Danny loved to fish, and that was one reason he liked the outdoors. He met a girl there, and they started dating. Danny and his girlfriend never got married, but she did come to Columbus to have their baby. They moved in with me for about a year. During that time, she had her baby, a girl named Jessie. But Danny's girlfriend became restless, and she and Jessie moved back to Portsmouth, Ohio, with her parents. Neither one of them knew what was needed to have a healthy marriage or even just a healthy relationship. When she found out that I had an African American boyfriend, she would no longer let Jessie come to my house.

Even though Danny loved his baby Jessie, he didn't have a job at that time, so with no income it was hard for him to go see her very much. The baby's grandmother told Jessie that her father didn't want her and neither did his family. That must have been so sad for Jessie. Danny and I called Jessie many times, but neither she or her mother would call us back or even message us back. When it was time for Jessie's high school graduation, her mother called me and asked me if I would be Jessie's grandma at her graduation party. I told her I had always been her grandmother but wasn't allowed to see her or even talk to her. That turned out to be the last time Danny or I got to see Jessie or even talk to her. We heard she went to college out of state. She is probably married and has children by now, children Danny and I will never get to see or know.

Later on, Danny met and married a girl named Casey. The whole family really liked her. Danny and Casey had two darling little girls named Tori and Taylor. I was able to give both of the girls their middle names, and that made me very happy and proud to have been able to do that. Shortly after the second baby was born, their marriage started going downhill. They were better friends than as a married couple.

Danny was close to the girls when they were growing up. Once they were old enough to drive, they went to visit their dad at his apartment. They always had a good time with him. Sometimes they would bring friends with them. One of their friends was named Lindsay. Lo and behold, she and Danny became boyfriend and girlfriend, even though he was quite a bit older than her. She was nineteen and he was forty-eight. That made it very hard for their relationship to last, but a beautiful baby girl was born from that relationship. They named her Scarlet Grae after Ohio State, whose colors are scarlet and gray. Danny loves the Buckeyes. She looked exactly like Danny's baby pictures, especially the freckles on her nose. Scarlet is now ten years old and still beautiful.

During this same time, Lindsay, Tori, and Taylor began using pain pills. Lindsay was able to quit, but Tori and Taylor couldn't, and they got progressively worse. Even the girls' mother, Casey, got addicted. Last year, Casey overdosed and died. She was an amazing woman who was too young to die. This became a crisis in our family that lasted way too long.

Tori, Taylor, and Devan are all doing well with their lives, and I am so very proud of them. David, Timmy, and Danny have survived all their problems with their kids. I shouldn't be surprised. They followed in my footsteps—having babies and a thousand marriages. Bobby and David never married. Danny is also an assistant manager at a large grocery chain.

My Daughter Tracena

When Tracena was born, we were going to name her Tracy, but we had a neighbor girl with that name, so we used Tracy as a nickname, and her real name was Tracena. Her brothers loved her and babied her, but when she got older, they were hard on her. But she had her own way of getting back at them.

Eddie, their dad, coached the four older boys on a football team that was called The Jets. They had white uniforms with green stripes.

I had to soak the boys' uniforms in the bathtub to get the mud out before I could put them in the washer.

Tracena was only two years old, but she was the Jets' cheerleader for our older boys' football team. She also had a white skirt and a blouse with green stripes. She didn't like being the cheerleader; she wanted to play sports with her brothers. Yes, she became a little tomboyish as she got older. I wanted to dress her up in frilly dresses, but she wanted to dress like her brothers.

When she started kindergarten, she wore jeans, a flannel shirt, and tennis shoes. As she grew up, she was really into sports. First, she played soccer for a few years and, along the way, started playing softball. In high school, she was on the softball team and played catcher. All my kids were good at sports. The boys were lucky that their father Eddie was their coach for football and basketball.

When Tracena was three years old, she wanted to take gymnastics. I enrolled her in a class close to home. She did really well in anything she pursued. Tracena was very smart in school and got very good grades. She now has a bachelor's and a master's degree.

Tracena had a son Cameron when she was twenty years old. When Cameron was two years old, she met a man at work and later married him. He had two daughters who he treated like princesses when they came over on the weekends. They could do anything they wanted. But Cameron had to be really well-behaved. Tracena's husband treated Cameron like he was invisible and was really strict with him. That marriage didn't last long.

Tracena and Cameron moved in with me, she went back to college, and Cameron went to daycare while she went to school. Then she would pick him up at daycare and bring him to the hospital where she was working the three-to-eleven shift as a unit clerk. I was already there, ending my seven-to-three shift as a nurse. I would take Cameron home with me and take care of him until she got off work. This was our routine for a few years.

Later, she ran into a man named Tom. They grew up in the same neighborhood. He had his son Jerry with him, as he had custody of him. Tracena and Tom soon married. Tom was a good father to Jerry and Cameron. Tom and Tracena had a son named Tommy, who was born in 2002. Tom and Tracena bought a new home, but they lost it when they divorced.

Tracena had to move in with me again, along with Cameron and Tommy. Jerry stayed with his dad. During this time, I got very close to Cameron and Tommy. I felt more like a second mother than that of a grandma. Tracena worked for the City Taxation Department and also went back to school to get her master's degree. It would be hard to say anything bad about Tracena. She was easier to take care of than the boys,

Bobby, David, Timmy, and Danny because when they were growing up there were four boys to one girl.

My Fifth Son Eddie Joe

Eddie Joe practically raised himself. I was in school and then working, and his dad was out of the picture. He did a great job on his own. He is a schoolteacher, an author, married with a good wife, and has twin sons who are now in college and are good Christian men.

Eddie was a teacher at an almost all-African-American high school. He was also the coach for the girls' varsity softball team. For these girls, their hopes and dreams had been broken with only a couple of weeks left in their first winning season in many years. Eddie had false accusations made against him for having an ineligible player. According to the rule book, she was eligible to play, but according to the Athletic Director, the rule can be interpreted differently. It depends on how the superiors want it to be interpreted to prove their point. There were also accusations against him that he was racist. How can you be a racist when your wife is African American? While all these accusations could be argued and debated for a long time, who had been totally forgotten? The girls.

Never mind that my son Eddie and his wife, Tonya, with their five-year-old twins, stayed after school every night for practice and games, even though they lived out of town an hour away. Never mind that he brought food all the time for the girls and provided transportation for them. Never mind that 99 percent of the time, none of them had parents at their games; their parents did not support them and basically had no involvement with the team whatsoever. Never mind that Eddie devoted himself totally as a coach and mentor for the team. None of that seemed to matter.

They were a completely frustrated team last year, but this year, the girls were eager and enthusiastic and excited about playing. They were starting to have pride in their team. Several may have been qualified for scholarships. Eddie was fired unjustly just two weeks prior to the girls' big game. When he was fired, he was told he couldn't coach for at least two more years, and then he could "ask" to coach once again. This was a devastating blow to the girls and Eddie. This is a man who takes pride and dedication in everything he does. Yes, he's my son, and I am not saying he is perfect. But I can say a couple of things about him about which I have no doubt. He does not cheat, and he does not lie. The varsity team was full of great young women who could have had a winning season, paving the way for a city championship. This would have been a successful start to adulthood.

Also, much appreciation to Tonya, my daughter-in-law, who was also invested in the varsity team, giving time and food, and being a friend to the girls. They now have a new coach who has never coached before. Once he became coach, the girls never won another game.

The four months Eddie coached, he showed dedication and a developing pride, a rising spirit, and a feeling of accomplishment for himself, his school, and his team. Abruptly and painfully, it was taken from him. Do the school administrators even care about what they have taken away from the varsity team and the girls?

Eddie left that school and got a teaching job at a Christian school. He wrote a book about the failing Columbus school system. His wife Tonya is also a teacher. She was at the same school and left there to get another teaching job. She is a good Christian woman. They both did a good job of raising their twin boys.

Joseph and Edward, the twins, volunteered their time to coach flag football for a church program.

Joseph and Edward played soccer, football, basketball, and baseball. They have been scholar-athletes since they started school. They have never had as much as a speeding ticket. In all their years in elementary and high school, they only had a total of two detentions. They are both now second-year students at their respective universities—Joseph at Notre Dame and Edward at Waynesburg University. Both boys earned full-tuition scholarships.

When the twins were born prematurely, Joseph's mother, Tonya, was told by the nurse in NICU that he wouldn't live so she might as well hold him before they sent him to surgery. With a lot of prayers, Joseph survived with a colostomy bag he had to wear for a while. The bag was later removed, and he was left with a permanent scar.

Joseph and Edward were supposed to be behind intellectually and physically, but both boys ended up testing as gifted.

Because their parents lived in the country, an hour away from their work, the boys spent a lot of time living with their grandparents (Tonya's parents) in the inner city. So, they split their time living the country life and the big city life in Columbus, Ohio.

The most popular phrase mentioned about the twins was that "they are good kids."

Chapter 13: My Parents

I have been talking a lot about my kids, grandkids, and great-grandkids. Now I want to introduce you to my parents and then some family updates.

My parents, Elvin and Cleo, are both deceased. My father was born in 1912 and passed away in 2000 at eighty-seven years old. He thought it would be a milestone in his life if he could live to welcome a new millennium, and he did. My dad coached the softball team for his church for many years and also played on the church Dartball team. He was loved by all of the family and many friends.

My mother was born in 1914 and passed away in 2013. She went to Heaven quietly in her sleep. She was ninety-eight years old. She was a Christian mother who had four daughters. She played the piano for her Sunday school class and, when needed, played the organ for her church. For two years, she led the church choir and accompanied them on the organ. She played for weddings, including two of her grandchildren's.

My mother learned to play the piano by ear. Just give her a song, and she was able to play the music to it on the piano and she could also play boogie-woogie. She played for numerous plays at church. Her favorite was the Hee Haw band, made up of people in the church. They went to different places in central Ohio to play for square dances.

Her greatest happiness was playing for her daughters, who sang for many years as a quartet, then a trio, and then a duo. When we sang for church events, everyone's favorite songs were "He Touched Me," "Surely Goodness and Mercy," and "There is Something About That Name." After a few years, two of my sisters moved. One moved out of the state, and one moved to another city. So only Suzi and I were able to sing as a duo. She sang soprano and I sang alto. At first, the four daughters were very shy when we sang in front of people, but eventually, we got over it. It was for our mother's happiness, and we really enjoyed it too. She was loved by all the family and many friends.

All my actions in my life were because I made many poor decisions and acted selfishly with my thoughts and behaviors. I was then, and I'm now taking accountability for all my actions. My parents were great role models, and I was blessed to have them. My oldest sister, Arline, who is now eighty-eight years old, had nine children: six boys and three girls. Suzi had two boys and one girl. Kay had two boys and one girl. And I have five boys and one girl.

Chapter 14: Friends in My Life

I have had three very special friends throughout my life. Patty and I have been friends since junior high school. Patty had to drop out of junior high school when she got pregnant. After she had her baby boy, I felt bad for her because I figured she'd have to be pretty lonely, being at home all the time, away from her friends, and just the normal things teenagers do. Most of her friends had forgotten about her after what happened. All that time we were only acquaintances. I got permission from my mother to go visit her and her baby. I can remember getting on the bus to go to her house and thinking maybe she needed a friend. She was only fourteen when she got pregnant. When it happened, we became close friends in about a year. We found that we had a lot in common. I got pregnant when I was fifteen, and I turned sixteen in June and had Bobby in July.

Patty and I kept in touch through our marriages, divorces, and some serious issues with our eldest sons. Patty's second son also got involved with some terrible problems. Both of her sons and my one son were in and out of prison. Most of it was because they had entered the whores of the farmer pharmacy world.

I won't give a running report of both of Patty's sons' deaths, but I can say that their deaths were associated with drugs. Tommy, her youngest son, died in 2003, and Mike, the oldest son, died recently in 2020. Patty was with Mike only minutes before he died. He was sitting on the side of the bed while they were talking. She left to go home, and on her way, she started thinking she felt something weird, so she turned around and went back to Mike's house. She found him lying on his back, where he had been sitting on the bed, died, and fell backward.

Patty was left only with memories and two holes in her heart. Personally, I feel she hasn't gotten over their deaths, and I wish I could help her. I also had problems dealing with my son's death, and I tend to hide my feelings behind walls. Patty does have a daughter who has been her salvation. She's a great woman and understands the pain her mother has endured. She also has to live with the loss. It was her two brothers who died.

Patty and I are still best friends. even though we don't see each other very often. We talk on the phone at least three or four times a week. She has a husband who takes up a lot of her time and rightfully so.

I also have another best friend, Nerissa, who I've worked with for many years. That was when we were RNs working in the hospital on the cancer floor. She was from Hong Kong. She always gave me support when I needed it, which was often. Nerissa was the smartest, most caring, and compassionate woman, and she was the one person you could ever hope to be your friend. Oh yes, I almost forgot to say, she's the best person in the hospital when it comes to starting an IV, even better than the doctors. I really do admire her. We have a lot of things in common. Especially, we both loved our patients.

Another friend I treasure, Kayla. She and I met at a bus stop waiting to go to night school. We had babies born a month apart. We had a lot in common and became good friends. She was married and her husband was in the Vietnam War. Before he left, they were discussing getting a divorce. They did, so that made both of us single mothers. Neither one of us had a social life or got to be a teenager. We were too busy having children and everything that goes along with that. I was married to Jace at the time and had babies before I ever had a date. The only way I could be around boys was to lie to my mother and sneak around. My mother never liked the boys that I chose in my life. I can see why now. Kayla and I became very close. We confided in each other. We supported each other in everything.

Kayla and I decided to go to a club one night, actually a bar. That's where I met the married man I wrote about earlier. He was the opposite of every other man that I had known. He was so kind and gentle, but I was also so disappointed because he could only see me a few times a month. When he was drinking, he said that was the only time he couldn't say no to quit seeing me. After a while, when he said he couldn't leave his kids, I knew he meant he couldn't leave his wife. I knew our relationship was over and that I had been so selfish and blind. So, to get over him, I moved out of the area. I knew when he was drinking, he wouldn't drive very far. It worked, and it seemed like it was only a dream. Although he did provide me companionship, a sense of belonging, and he boosted my confidence. I felt desirable and loved. Wow, this was a hard lesson. I will never forget how I prayed for forgiveness for these wrongs that I did at that time in my life. Thank God, He does forgive us.

My girlfriend Kayla was with me and gave me hope for a good future. She was always there for me.

Kayla remarried and moved to southern Ohio and became a foster mother. She ended up adopting three children. When her oldest daughter was sixteen, she was out with two boys, riding around in a pickup truck. They had a wreck. She was sitting in the middle with no seat belt on, so she was thrown out of the windshield from the impact. She only lived for three days after that. Kayla, her family, and her many friends, including me, were heartbroken. We rarely see each other, but we do keep in contact.

Another friend was Francine. We met at work, and we got to know each other. We never went out because she had a husband, but we talked a lot on the phone. Later on, she worked at the CVS drugstore. She worked at another hospital for a while, but it was too many hours to work, so she just kept her CVS job. She liked to travel a lot. Francine had two daughters who were good girls who never got in trouble. Her oldest daughter passed away recently at the age of thirty-one. She died of an aneurysm. Francine knows that we are all here for her.

My new friend I want to mention is my daughter's housekeeper, Nichole. We got to know each other while she cleaned. I didn't want to distract her, so I only talked to her while she was working in the kitchen and I was eating lunch or dinner. Hopefully, we will get to know each other better as time goes on.

Chapter 15: Updates

I now have thirteen grandchildren and ten great-grandchildren.

My children and grandchildren:

Bobby, no children.

David 60,1 son: J.R. 37. And 2 grandchildren: Nicholas 17, MacKenzie 14.

Timmy 58, 4 children: Emily 37, Tyler 35, Devan 33, Autumn 30.

Seven grandchildren: Lincoln 14, Landon 10, Lawson 4, Maylene 7, Macy 5, Lucy 5, Sunny 1.

Danny 57, 4 children: Jessie 37, Tori 31, Taylor 29, Scarlett 10.

Tracena 53, 2 children and 1 stepson: Jerry 30, Cameron 33, Tommy 21,

One granddaughter: Brezzy 2 1/2 (Cameron's daughter).

Eddie Joe 50, 2 children: Joseph 20, Edward 20.

David's grandkids are living with him temporarily. Timmy shares a home with David. Timmy doesn't get to see his kids and grandkids very often, because they all live out of town. Timmy's two daughters,

Devan and Autumn, keep in touch with each other. They would like to get the whole family together next summer for a family reunion. That would really be nice, as some of the cousins don't even know each other.

Danny gets to see his kids because they live close to him, but he still doesn't get to see them a lot. One reason Danny can't see his kids much is because his car is ready to go to the junkyard. It was originally my car, and I bought it new in 2003. It was my very first new car. Danny has driven it for a few years. Danny doesn't have any grandchildren, unless his oldest daughter Jessie has children he doesn't know about. All three of my sons like their beer, but that's their choice. They all three have good jobs.

Now to Tracena, my only daughter. I have to say that she really takes good care of me. I had some issues when I retired, and that caused me to cry uncontrollably. So, I went to see a psychiatrist. He put me on some medications to try to even out my emotions, and he diagnosed me with severe anxiety and panic attacks and, of course, depression. I am fairly good now, and Tracena does watch out for me. Sometimes she gets aggravated with me, but it's hard to listen to your daughter when you're the mother, even though I know she's doing it for my own good. She gives me things to do that are safe. She doesn't want me to go outside unless someone is with me, because I fall a lot.

In fact, a year ago, I fell in my bedroom against the end of my bed and broke eight ribs. Two of them were broken in two places, and one of them punctured one of my lungs. Now, I have a lot of plates and screws in my body. After I was home for a couple of days, I got pneumonia and had to go back to the hospital. It was very painful, and it took me a few months to recover.

Tracena's two sons are fine. Her oldest son, Cameron, lives in Florida, and he has a daughter who is two and a half years old. They call her Breezy. Tracena just loves her to death, and she goes to visit her about three or four times a year. Her youngest son, Tommy, just graduated from college, and he got a really good job.

Tommy won some awards while he was in college. The last one he got just recently is supposedly the most prestigious award at Miami University except for valedictorian: Provost Student Award for Academic Achievement.

He and his girlfriend have a nice apartment. They got a dog named Murphy in their last semester. Tommy said Murphy has grown a lot and is crazy. Tracena's stepson, Jerry, is also doing well.

Tracena is a newlywed, so we have been moving a lot. I have moved four times in the last four years. There are always reasons why we move, but I told her this is the last time for me. It is usually to get a bigger house. We will be moving back to Gahanna on September 1, 2023. This is our fourth house.

My daughter married a very nice and good man named Mark. He is the love of her life. They just bought a big house, and I have a bedroom, bathroom, and a living room.

Now to my youngest son, Eddie Joe. He does not like beer, and he does not drink or smoke. He and his wife, Tonya, are very devout Christians. They go to church every week and have raised their twin boys in the church. Tonya has a very pretty voice and leads the singing at her church. Eddie Joe and Tonya always monitored what the boys watched on television and the music they listened to. They kept the twins busy with sports. Eddie, my son, coached a lot of their sports. The boys played soccer, baseball, basketball, and football. Eddie coached them much the same as his father used to do for him and his brothers. The twins are now nineteen years old, and they are both in college. They are great kids. Any time I call them to help me, they come over. Among other things, they dig holes for me so I can plant my crepe myrtles, my favorite bushes with beautiful flowers.

I have to say that Cameron, Tommy, Edward, and Joseph are very close to me because they have spent a lot of time with me. I feel like I know them better than my other grandchildren. I would sure like to get to know all of them better because that's a blessing for a grand-mother—to love and be able to be loved back by her grandchildren and great-grandchildren. Eddie and Tonya are both schoolteachers. They taught in a school that was in a ghetto. They had shootings and a lot of fights outside the school and hardly anybody graduated from that school or even attended much. Eddie and Tonya were very strong teachers who would not falsify anything for their students, and for that, I'm very proud of them.

All my boys will do anything I need them to do. I just have to ask them. I know they get tired of me asking for transportation because I don't want to drive anymore since I have so much anxiety. So, I appreciate everything they do for me, and I hope I raised them to what my goal was. I told myself when I had children, I wanted to teach all of them about Jesus and God and to be true believers.

Chapter 16: My Ending: Battling with Depression

How do you write an ending to a story that started seventy-seven years ago? It isn't easy because for every action there is a reaction. Now, I have the best reaction to every calamity in my life. A lot of the time, I had no outward reactions at all in the course of my life. I started with an innocent heart. In time, I went on to become more like a robot with suppressed emotions in order to be conceived of as strong and able to handle all the hurt, guilt, hopelessness, and feelings of being totally solo. I've had to control favorable outcomes of every situation. Everybody told me how strong I was and how well I handled adversity, but they were so wrong. Internally, I was only numb and had no idea how to continue on. Did I cause a lot of my problems? Yes, but not intentionally. When my husband shot a stranger on the freeway and then told the police that he had a deep-seated hatred for all women—how was I supposed to feel and how was I supposed to react? I just wanted a father for my son. At the time, I didn't realize that was not a good reason to marry him.

How was I supposed to react when I wasted ten years of my life for a murderous prisoner? I saw some red flags, but I thought he just needed someone to love him and support him emotionally and financially. I thought he was the love of my life only because I needed him. I was insecure and didn't feel any worth. I worked hard to get him out of prison. He said I was the last priority on his to-do list. When he got out, I did everything to make him happy. New clothes, money, a job, and a decent home. In return, I got nothing. He wouldn't even touch me, hold me, kiss me, or have sex. Nothing! In six weeks, he moved out and had never even kissed me.

One night he brought his girlfriend to my house and said, "Isn't she pretty?" They were both drunk and high, and then he added that he was able to have sex with her. Why did he bring her to my house? To make me feel ugly, not attractive enough for sex, and unloved?

The next thing I knew, Alva turned to robbery for drugs and then finally murdered an eighteen-year-old boy for his truck. He no longer had his girlfriend, who was only with him the first three months he was out. How was I supposed to feel? How was I supposed to react? I've learned from my many mistakes, but it took me a long time.

During the ten years I waited for Alva, I became a different person. I had a different mindset. I could hope for my unknown future. I felt lucky to have found a tarnished but great human being who needed a chance to be loved. I thought I could help him by loving him and changing him of any imperfections he possessed. Alva had a good institutional record. He told me about his good record of conduct, and that he was a trusted and hard worker. After about five or six years, he got a job in an office at the prison and had a lot of responsibility. He was active in a program called

"Scared Straight." He was one of the speakers talking to selected troubled kids. They were preteens and teenagers who had problems with bad behavior at home and in school. They had problems with breaking the law. The kids were filled with anger, and many came from dysfunctional families. They listened to the inmates talk about their lives and how they ended up in prison, some of them with life sentences.

The program is intended to scare the kids into being good citizens, to change their lives around, and to change their mindsets. A lot of times, there were favorable results, but some of them ended up in prison or dead. Some of the kids didn't seem easily scared, but some of them really were "scared straight." Sometimes this program also helped the inmates.

I'm so blessed to have a supporting and loving family, even though I brought stress and confusion to my home. I love my kids with all my heart, my mending heart. I love my grandkids and my great-grandkids so much.

My life has still been like an emotional roller coaster. I'm still learning from my weak decisions. I'm still learning how to love myself. I also have a lot of good things in my life, but I'm still on the side of the (Fjord) cliff, afraid of falling in the water and drifting out to sea. But I know with God's help, he'll keep me out of the water. He's beside me now and always has been. That's how I survived.

Alva's prosecutor said that he was the perfect poster person to represent the death penalty. Finally, Alva did confess to his crimes and was given the death penalty. While struggling with my emotions, the guilt, the hurt, and the sorrow for him taking a young man's life will never leave my mind. Now how am I supposed to feel?

Chapter 17: A Personal Letter to Myself

My head is hurting in this mess of confusion and feels like a top going around in circles. I don't feel capable of solving my problems or making any decisions right now. This spinning needs to stop so I can concentrate. It makes me anxious and sad. I have a lot on my mind and, evidently, I tried to block the anxiety with music or humming noises. I feel like I am on the verge of a panic attack. At different periods of the day, I would think of a song, and later I would think of a different song. I can't concentrate. Motrin quieted the music turning in my head, then it came back worse than before. I felt so out of control in my brain that I decided it would be best if I took my nighttime pills and went to bed. I wasn't even able to watch the Lakers, my favorite basketball team. Silence, please.

After four and a half years, I was finally able to cry. But it's more like a silent cry with only a few tears. I try to make myself cry harder, thinking it may stop the top spinning in my head and give me relief from some of my anxieties. It just doesn't happen.

After praying about my life being in a time of upheaval, I realized that God would keep me out of the water.

What do I want? In my life: To write books that will help others, to support and acknowledge, and to overcome whatever comes my way. I want to have the love of God guide and direct my life. I want to pray for my enemies, to know that I am a child of God, and He loves and cares about me just as I am.

What do I want? With my family: 1. To have total honesty. 2. To make amends. 3. To give more of my heart and my time.

What do I want? With my job: I wanted to be appreciated for my hard work. I wanted to be respected for my experience and wisdom.

45 Wishes for Myself and My Family. I started this list on July 5, 2012, and added to it as each child was born.

1. To be physically healthy.

2. To go to Heaven.

3. For David, Timmy, and Danny to quit smoking.

4. For David, Timmy, and Danny to quit smoking pot.

5. For David, Timmy, and Danny to quit drinking.

6. For Eddie Joe to quit using the internet that's expressing damning information.

7. For Tracena to have a good man she can trust.

8. To see the twins more.

9. For JoJo and Edward to accept being individuals.

10. For Edward to feel he is loved and is not second best.

11. For Tommy to excel in everything he does.

12. For Nick to be safe.

13. For Mackenzie to be safe.

14. For Nick to know that his dad loves and misses him.

15. For Mackenzie to know that her dad loves and misses her.

16. For David to continue loving them and being a good influence.

17. For J.R. (Nick and McKenzie's dad) to quit drugs, see his kids, and live a fruitful life.

18. For Tori to have a successful life and be drug-free.

19. For Taylor to be drug-free and have control of her life.

20. For Devon to be drug-free and have control of her life.

21. For Terry to be drug-free and have control of his life.

22. For Scarlett to be back in our family and be close to Danny.

23. For Autumn and her baby, Sunny, to be in our family and be close to Timmy.

24. For Jerry to feel a part of our family.

25. For Edward, JoJo, and Tommy to feel close and not be competitive.

26. For Mother to die peacefully, hopefully in her sleep.

27. To have my selected music played at my funeral.

28. For Cameron to come to the point of realization of self.

29. For Cameron to be independent.

30. For Cameron to have a good job.

31. For Cameron to have a good future.

32. For Cameron to know his father loves him but has limitations.

33. For Cameron to get a good education.

34. For Cameron to have his dreams fulfilled.

35. For all of my grandchildren to follow their dreams.

36. To find my place in this life.

37. To be a good example to everyone in my family.

38. To leave a meaningful legacy when I die.

39. To have a new closeness with all three sisters.

40. For all my family to believe in God and Jesus.

41. For all my family to go to Heaven.

42. For all my children to live healthy lives.

43. For Suzi's health to improve.

44. To forget my past incidents and forgive myself.

45. To forgive those involved in my past who abused me and hurt me.

Chapter 18: Finding My Way Home

As I look back on the pages of my life, I see a journey that began with the simple joys of a carefree childhood, where love and laughter were my constant companions. But as I grew older, the harsh realities of life began to unfold, revealing a world that was far more complex and challenging than the innocent eyes of youth could have foreseen.

From a young age, I sought love with a fervent hope that it would fill the voids and heal the scars that life had slowly etched upon my heart. I believed that creating a family of my own would bring the fulfillment I so desperately craved. Yet, even surrounded by the children I adored, a part of me continued to seek love elsewhere, hoping to find it in the arms of partners who often brought more pain than solace.

My journey through love was fraught with missteps and heartache. I walked down the aisle multiple times, each marriage a testament to my longing for a connection that would endure. But each union, in its turn, peeled back layers of myself I had to confront—my fears, my hopes, and the unresolved wounds from my past.

But every heartbreak, every disappointment, was not in vain. The trials I faced were not just obstacles; they were lessons that taught me the hardest truth of all—that the love I was searching for in others needed to come from within. My path to self-love was long and arduous, filled with many days where the light seemed just out of reach.

Yet, it is with a heart full of gratitude that I now recognize the most profound love was guiding me all along. The grace and mercy of the Lord were my beacons in the darkest times, leading me to discover that the greatest love of all is the love that comes from our Father in Heaven.

This book is not just my story. It is a message to anyone who might find themselves lost in the shadows of their trials, searching for a beacon. Remember, what you endure is never just for you—it is a testament of strength and resilience meant to guide others through their storms.

As you close this book, I hope you carry away a smile and the knowledge that I made it through. My life now stands as a testament to enduring love and faith, a reminder that no matter how tough the journey, we are never walking alone.

ALVA BEFORE

ALVA CAMPBELL
1982

ALVA CAMPBELL
1982
SHAROL KELLY

ALVA CAMPBELL
1982
Sharol's son's Danny, E.J. & Bobby

ALVA CAMPBELL
1987
SHAROL, KELLY

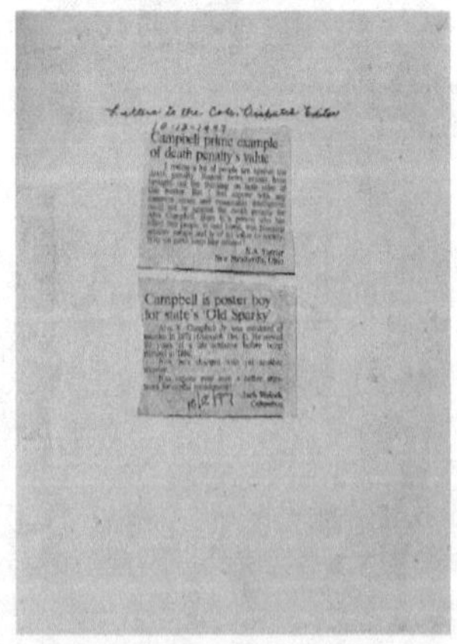

MY LIFE AS IT STANDS

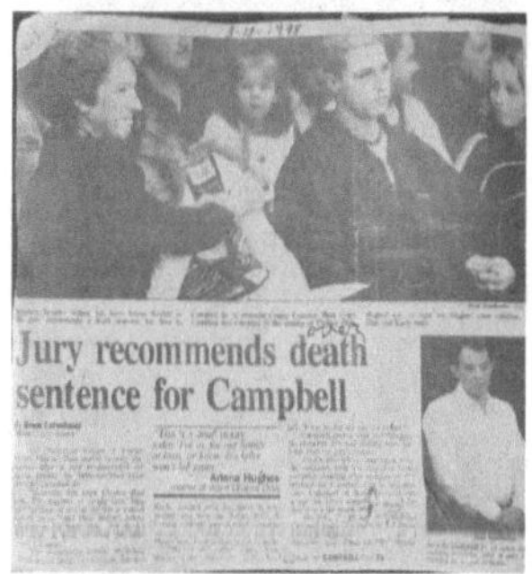

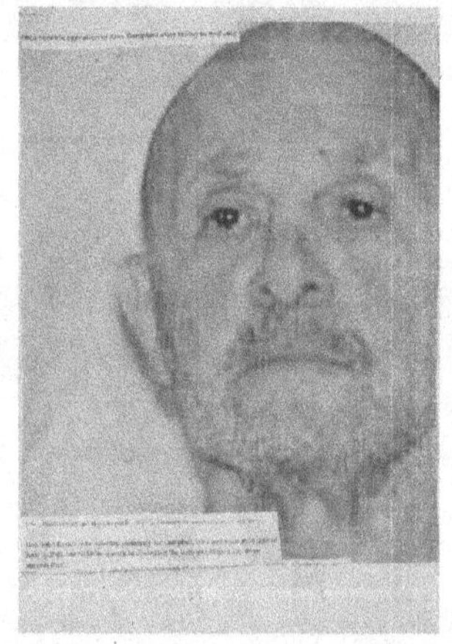

Acknowledgement

My sister Susie made it possible for me to write my book. She wasmy typist and my spelling guru. She made sense of my ideas. She was able to fill in some blanks when I couldn't. I will finish by saying I can describe her in one word and that's the manager.

Next is Tonya Temple. She deserves a big thank you. Tonya had good ideas and gave good support. She teaches at a high school as does her husband Eddie who I would like to acknowledge next.

Eddie Temple is my youngest son, and he needs to be given thanks because he gave me a lot of tips on publishing a book as he has published a few. His best advice was to introduce me to Ashequka Lacey a former student of his and that was awesome.

Sheq Lacey has also published a couple of books. She was a mentor to me and soon became my teacher. She taught me about the process of getting a book published, but she did everything for me. What needed completing, she did all of the legwork and all of the technical jobs. Most importantly she gave me, a lot of her precious time she was an excellent teacher. I'm truly humbled.

Next are David Temple, Timmy Temple, and Danny Temple. These are three of my sons and they inspired me a lot. They gave me encouragement and supported me.

Finally, Tracena and her husband, Mark, whom I live with, had to deal with my mood swings a lot of questions, and my constant talking about the book. For that reason, she highly encouraged me to finish the book and set her free. My 13 grandchildren and great great grandchildren also deserve a thank you for asking questions with few answers and keeping me grounded.

About the author

I started nursing school and worked as an RN for 30 years. The last 10 years I worked with cancer patients they offered office visits and gave chemotherapy, I love the patience but not too much for the management. I spend my time in the garden with flowers and bushes especially the crêpe myrtleI have a dog she is a Yorky, which in case you don't know is a mix of a Maltese and Yorkshire terrier. Her name is Rain and she is my best friend, I am 78 years old now and I love life. The end.